Shanghai Deliverance

A Holocaust Survival Story

How Hope, Faith, Love and Good Fortune
Saved my Family

Edie Shafer

As Told by Edie Shafer

Written by Mary Munson Murphy
with Sara Sillars

Book Design by Liz Townsend

Printed in the United States of America
Shafer Publishing

ISBN: 978-0-615-91801-3

Dedicated to my parents and my grandfather who survived the Holocaust and to those of our family who did not.

First Jews were categorized; then civil liberties were restricted and property confiscated. Next, Jews were dismissed from universities and civil service jobs, which often included school teaching, and were barred from the professions. Jewish businesses were taken over and Aryanized. Jews were then isolated, forced to wear the Jewish star and forbidden to use public facilities.

Finally Jews were assembled, first in large cities and then in transit camps. From 1942 on, they were deported from these transit camps to the death camps in the east.

The event is the Holocaust - the systematic state-sponsored murder of six million Jews by the Nazis and their collaborators during World War II.

- *From* The World Must Know: The History of the Holocaust as Told in the United States Holocaust Memorial Museum - *Michael Berenbaum*

Remember gratefully your earliest childhood in Shanghai. At the time of worst distress and danger of life, when all gates of the whole world were closed for us, Shanghai was the only place, which gave refuge and secured the living for your parents and for thousands [sic] of other Jews.

- Max Kuba

Acknowledgements

Being born in the Shanghai Ghetto has played a significant role in who I am. Many miracles needed to happen in order for me to be here today.

Whether one believes such miracles just happen because of luck or good fortune, or through a higher power, is an individual preference. I believe in G-d and am very thankful for everything I have.

I start by thanking the two people who have actually worked so hard to bring this book to completion, Mary Munson Murphy and Sara Sillars. Both are truly caring and understanding people. The idea for the cover came from them. Cindy Cooper took this idea and created a marvelous and meaningful cover image.

Mary's husband, Terry, also deserves a word of thanks for his strong support of Mary and the entire project.

A very special word of appreciation goes to Lyn Knight for his generous offer to print and produce this book.

Liz Townsend, Graphic Design specialist, did an outstanding job with the overall presentation. I am deeply grateful for her work on this book.

I always wanted a family; now I have three grown children and their spouses, and eight grandchildren, the joys of my life. In order of age they are Shoshi, Rachel, Yoni, Alex, Sam, Katie, Golan and Eli. I love them all!!

They are the real reason why I wanted this book. My husband of almost 50 years has also been very supportive of this book in every way possible, and I thank him for making it a reality.

Edie Shafer

Table of Contents

"Was her friend Jewish?
I knew that family. I held that baby."

Shanghai Ghetto, 2010: Mary Munson Murphy, standing with a woman who knew Edie's parents and held her when she was a baby. Nel Brouwer photo.

Preface

Mary Munson Murphy

I first visited the Shanghai Ghetto area, formerly officially designated as the Restricted Sector for Stateless Refugees, long before I met Edie Shafer through our mutual work for the Nathan and Esther Pelz Holocaust Education Resource Center (HERC), located in Milwaukee, Wisconsin. I worked there as its educator as I had for Holocaust Museum Houston, located in Houston, Texas. Edie chaired the HERC Operations Committee and was a member of our Speakers Bureau so I knew she was a Holocaust survivor, but I did not know her history.

When I told her I was traveling to China with my husband who was going on a business trip, she told me that she was born there in 1941. She asked if I would visit the Ghetto area and search for her birthplace.

She vividly recalled its location, 161 Chusan Road, just across from a large prison, enclosed by an immense wall. I promised to do my best. Armed with the address, a photo of their place, and the help of Nel Brouwer, a Dutch friend of mine who spoke Mandarin, I set off to find what Edie needed - an update on where she was born.

At first Nel and I searched the streets, hopelessly. The Ghetto streets were narrow except for countless main thoroughfares. Everywhere street vendors sold fresh fish and other difficult-to-identify foods. Bicyclists and walkers weaved in and out as we navigated the area.

The prison Edie remembered was our beacon and finally, with great jubilation, we found it. There was a corner shop at 161 Chusan Road, just where Edie said it would be. Nel, my trusty friend and translator, asked permission from its new owner to photograph the shop. After Nel explained that I wanted the photo for a friend born there, the owner quickly agreed.

Meanwhile, people gathered to see what these two Westerners were doing. More miraculously, a tiny woman came from the end of the enclosed street that bordered the shop.

"Was her friend Jewish?"

"Yes, indeed."

That is when the woman told me the most astonishing thing of all: "I knew that family. I held that baby."

Holocaust historians and those who survived the Third Reich under Adolf Hitler by fleeing to Shanghai have preserved remarkable details about the Reich's twelve-year existence, from 1933 - 1945. Although critical to understanding life in pre-war Germany, post-*Kristallnacht* Germany, and life in the Shanghai Ghetto, individual stories of personal courage breathe life into this history.

The story of Edie Shafer and her family's journey from Germany to Shanghai and finally to America is one such story. Before her mother and father died, her husband Neil recorded a series of interviews with them. The resulting CDs provided me with first-hand accounts of their experiences. In the book whenever possible, I have quoted from those interviews. A full transcription of the interviews, completed by my colleague Sara Sillars, is located at the back of the book.

This memoir is intended as a tribute to remember family members lost in the Holocaust, not as a complete history of post-*Kristallnacht* experience in Shanghai. It honors Edie's parents and grandfather for their courage in the face of hardships. Their love for each other and for Edie, their new daughter born in the Ghetto, kept them steadfast in their unwavering hope and belief that survival was possible.

My mother and father the day before they married. Oelsner family photo.

Introduction

Putting the words, "Jews" and "Shanghai" in the same sentence is as unlikely in 2013 as it was when my father made the decision to move his family there from Germany in 1939, although there had been Jews in China as early as the 7th or 8th centuries. My parents were among the almost 18,000 Jews going to Shanghai to escape Nazi Germany as it was one of the very few places on Earth that would accept them.

This city in China, the world's most populous country today, is 5,300 miles from Germany. The culture was distinctly different from that in Germany, where my parents lived a simple life. In 1938, with love and courage, they married in spite of everything that was happening in Germany. Their love led the way.

The Nazis, however, had a very different future planned for them. Adolf Hitler came to power in 1933 when German President Paul von Hindenburg appointed him Chancellor of Germany. Even without absolute control, he and the Nazi Party moved quickly to consolidate their power and issue measures against the Jews and others. After Hindenburg died in 1934, Hitler controlled everything, issuing edicts against Jews that became harsher as the years passed.

Then in November of 1938, wide-spread violence against Jews (a pogrom) occurred in Germany and Austria. It became known as *Kristallnacht* or Night of Broken Glass. All across Germany and Austria, Nazis burned Jewish businesses and smashed windows while gangs of Nazi youths looted their stores. Synagogues were burned and Holy Scriptures, the Torah, were torched. Jews themselves were beaten and as many as 30,000 were arrested. German authorities heavily fined the Jewish people for the destruction leveled against them. *Kristallnacht* clearly signaled to many Jews that they must leave Germany.

Why go to Shanghai? It was about the only place on Earth that would accept Jews without visas. My parents were extremely lucky to have gotten out, even though they were going to a place so far away in distance and even further away culturally.

When my parents arrived there, they could not believe what they saw and smelled. They, along with my grandfather and 40 to 50 others, were quickly loaded onto an open flat-bed truck with sides that rose about eight inches.

"After living four weeks on the boat [A ship named the *Conte Verde*] in very luxurious conditions, we arrived in Shanghai," my father said. "I never in my life saw such a big contrast between the conditions on the boat and Shanghai."

They were quite sad, seeing that first experience as a sign of what was to come.

Life Before

"Be a Jew in your home and a man in the street."

- Well-known Jewish saying in Germany

"There was a love affair between Jews and Germans but it was one-sided: Jews loved Germany and Germans; Germans didn't love Jews, even if they didn't hate them. One-sided love affairs usually don't work well."

- Professor Yehuda Bauer, Hebrew University in Jerusalem

"We were so German. We didn't think it could happen to us."

- Gerda Oelsner

How did so many Jews come to feel German? Jews fought side by side with Germans during the Revolutions of 1848 (also known as the Spring of Nations, Spring Time of the Peoples, or the Year of Revolution). Jews and other revolutionaries stood with liberals who wanted to change the world, leading to recognition as full citizens. The results were ambiguous at best. Civil rights granted in the German states were quickly abolished as soon as the power of the monarchy was restored.

Finally with the unification of Germany and the final emancipation decree dated January 12, 1871, German Jewry became full citizens of the German Empire. Throughout the 19th century, Jews

7

in Germany (and elsewhere) advocated the adoption of more modern practices.

Many Jews in Germany saw the goal as a lifelong re-educating of themselves and other Jews to fit better into modern society. "Be a Jew in your home and a man in the street" was their motto.[1]

With their new status, German Jews participated fully in economic, political and cultural life. Jews could be found in every walk of life: farmers, tailors, factory hands, accountants, doctors, teachers, small-business owners, and yes, bankers, explains Susan D. Bachrach of the United States Holocaust Memorial Museum in Tell Them We Remember. As time went on, more Jews assimilated into German culture and identified themselves as Germans. They were Jewish, but the important part for many was they were Germans. For others, being Jewish was more important, but Germany was their country.

Despite reaching equality officially, an undercurrent of distrust existed, a remnant of long-held antisemitic prejudices. "There was a love affair between Jews and Germans but it was one-sided: Jews loved Germany and Germans; Germans didn't love Jews, even if they didn't hate them. One-sided love affairs usually don't work well," wrote Professor Yehuda Bauer of Hebrew University in Jerusalem. Jews were used for their contributions but were not accepted fully. They were not rejected but were not loved, according to Bauer.[2]

"In the decades following 1848 [The Year of Revolution], many Jews realized that social and economic emancipation depended less on legalization and more on the willingness of the population at large to accept Jews as fellow citizens," wrote Glenn R. Sharfman, Holocaust historian and Dean for Academic Affairs at Manchester University in Indiana.[3]

Acceptance became even tougher to achieve in the final decades of the 19th century. George L. Mosse said, "Patriotism, duty, and discipline threatened to replace the critical mind of the Enlightenment, a prerequisite for the self-cultivation of man."[4] Self-cultivation was replaced by conformity that isolated Jews even further. The new concept of Bildung was rooted in a shared historical past and shared cultural values embraced by the majority of Germans. As outsiders, Jews were easily marked as the "Other."

The place of German Jews became even more tenuous after World War I (WWI) because of the German loss and the ever-present reparations burden mandated by the Allies in the Treaty of Versailles. The deepening economic depression and a growing sense of uncertainty for all played into Hitler's hands. The Jews were the cause for the nation's economic woes, Hitler told his people.

A Nazi coup in the 1920s ended with disastrous results. Now their goal was to achieve power through legitimate channels and then restore Germany to what they considered its rightful place in the world. To achieve that goal the Nazis would deal with Jews and other state-defined enemies.

1933, It Begins

There was a time when life in Germany was good, not perfect, but good - the life before. My grandfather Max Kuba fought for Germany during World War I just like Otto Frank, Anne Frank's father. When the Nazi troubles began my mother, Gerda, said that they knew what Hitler had written in *Mein*

Kampf; however, she and many other Germans thought, "This will all blow over."

"We were so German," she said. "We didn't think it could happen to us."

My parents were just beginning their relationship when Hitler came to power in 1933 by being appointed chancellor of Germany. Gerda and Manfred met on June 26, 1932, through a connection between my grandparents, Max and Ida Kuba, and my father's aunt, all friends who spent their evenings and weekends walking together.

My father lived in Leipzig, an ancient trading city about 93 miles south of Berlin. My mother was in Forst-Lausitz, which is on the German-Polish border.

My father told me he periodically rode his bicycle to Forst-Lausitz, a journey of more than 150 miles to visit his aunt, but made the visit more often after meeting my mother. I'm not sure if he rode those 150 miles or took his bicycle on the train, only riding the final leg to his aunt's home.

My beautiful mother and my handsome father fell in love. Their courtship was simple: they visited families, traveled with families, and enjoyed long walks and interesting discussions. The time from when they met to the day and time of their marriage was exactly six years, to the moment.

My mother's parents owned and operated a general store where she sometimes worked. She continued her education through secondary school and later worked as a secretary. After her mother, my grandmother Ida, died in 1934, she continued to live with my grandfather, Max.

Manfred worked at a bowling alley in Leipzig where he

My father in kiosk at Nazi Bowling Club in Germany. Oelsner family photo.

My father's Nazi-issued Work Book.

sold tobacco products in a kiosk. He lost his job three weeks after Hitler became chancellor because he had to be a member of the Nazi Party and of course, Jews couldn't be members. Financial insecurity followed because he simply could not get permanent work. He actually worked at a Nazi club selling cigarettes and cigars. The doorman knew he was Jewish, but accepted him. My father knew the doorman was a Nazi but said, "You had to make a living."

While working at that club, Manfred decided to join his family for a vacation to the Baltic Sea. Mr. Abel, his boss, urged him not to go. "Fred, a situation is coming that will be troubled," he told my dad. "I can't keep your job but there is a table where you will always be able to eat."

My dad lost that job when he returned from his holiday but he said he was so exhausted, he just needed the rest. After that, he worked as a vacuum cleaner salesman going door-to-door soliciting sales, a job his brother also worked. "We had to salute and say 'Heil Hitler' just to get in the door," my father said. That job lasted only three or four months.

He then worked as a busboy in a restaurant owned by Jews. That ended around December of 1936 when one of the three brothers who owned the business tried to escape to Czechoslovakia, now the Czech Republic. After he was caught at the border, the restaurant was closed.

My father then moved from Leipzig to Forst-Lausitz to be near my mother, his fiancee. He managed to get a job as a general helper at a "credit store," what today would be an agency in charge of liquidations and past-due collections. He was a delivery boy at first. "I worked my way up and soon kept the books, and went to court when lawsuits were filed," he said. "I worried because the judge was a Nazi and knew I was Jewish, although nothing bad happened."

The Nazi Regime

"The Nazis wanted the Jews to emigrate so they arrested the men and said to the women, you'll get them back but you have to get out of Germany, in two weeks, three weeks, or a few months."

- Professor Irene Eber of Hebrew University, Jerusalem

"In mid-morning I opened the front door of our apartment and saw to my horror, two SS men standing there. I immediately closed the door [...] I think it was only ten minutes later that they knocked [again], told my husband that he is arrested, and took him away."

- Gerda Oelsner

"My feelings about when I arrived in that camp... it's a very, very hard thing to describe. You are coming out of normal living conditions [and] your normal privileges. You have, you had your freedom of speech, your freedom of thinking, your freedom of behavior, completely free to behave the way you are willing to. Then they are taking you first in that chair, then they are packing you in that truck, then they transport you to that concentration camp and there, there you see the walls and above the walls every fifty yards you see a little like a tower with a machine gun in there and above the walls you see the SS people patrolling and you are asking yourself out of nowhere, 'My gosh, what have I done? I'm not a gangster.' You are not

able to find an answer for this until you realize... you are a Jew and that is the only reason why."

- Manfred Oelsner

Life changed for all Germans under Hitler and the Nazis, but most especially for German Jews. Nazis publicly burned books in 1933, those written by Jews plus those written by others who criticized the Nazis and their policies. Random attacks occurred on Jews and on Jewish property. There was no recourse under law because the police and the courts no longer protected Jews or others deemed enemies of the state.

Actions against Jews, trade unionists, Communists, political dissidents and others occurred frequently in 1933 and 1934. (My mother told me that people were afraid to do or say anything because they "didn't know what the other guy was thinking.") Some wealthier people left when they had the chance. Others tried to convert to Christianity, but still were not accepted by the Nazis who went back generations to identify Jews.

Perhaps the most important event was the establishment of the Department of Racial Hygiene that grew out of an 1800s scientific and social phenomenon supposedly designed to control and perfect the human species. In 1881, Francis Galton, an English naturalist and mathematician first used the word eugenics, Greek for "good birth".

The so-called "science" of eugenics was popular in the United States as well as in Germany and other European countries. It consisted of a belief that promoted limiting or eliminating births of "inferiors" while increasing births among families deemed "valuable." It discussed "race-mixing" as a key to biological degeneration.[5]

Karl Binding, a German jurist, and Alfred Hoche, a German psychiatrist, published Die Freigabe der Vernichtung lebensunwerten Lebens (Authorization of the Destruction of Life Unworthy of Life) *in 1920. They argued that the best and brightest were sacrificed on the fields of battle while those with mental or physical deficiencies lived and depleted national resources, giving nothing back. The Nazis used their work to justify the Nazi T-4 program that euthanized the "hereditarily ill." Though Hitler had limited interest in the program, he referred to the disabled as "useless eaters."*[6]

Over the years the Nazis and the Third Reich enacted more and increasingly severe measures against the Jews of Germany. The measures excluded Jews from becoming doctors, lawyers, and entering other professions. Jewish doctors were banned from attending to the needs of all "Aryan" patients. Jews also were excluded from military service.

The Nuremberg Laws were enacted in 1935, stripping Jews of all civil rights. The Law for the 'Protection of German Blood and German Honor' forbade mixed marriages. This law and the earlier establishment of the Department for Racial Hygiene grew out of the Nazis' belief in the racial superiority of the Aryan race that they felt should be protected from contamination by contact with inferior races, most especially the Jews.

The list of other measures is too lengthy to detail here but they continued throughout the years of the Third Reich. Jews were ostracized and frightened even before the pogrom in 1938 called Kristallnacht, *or Night of Broken Glass, when it became clear that no Jew was safe under the Nazis.*

Pogroms, a Russian word meaning attack, had happened before in many other places, most notably Eastern Europe. The word came to be synonymous with "an organized riot and massacre of Jews with complicity of the authorities."[7] Non-Jews attacked Jews and stole or destroyed their possessions, taking any Jewish-owned property without fear of punishment.

On November 9-10, 1938, Kristallnacht *made all the earlier pogroms seem mild by comparison. Nazis ravaged Jewish communities throughout Germany and Austria as well as in the Sudetenland and Danzig. The excuse was retaliation for the slaying of Ernst vom Rath, third-secretary of the German Embassy in Paris.*

In 1938, Hitler threatened to unleash a European war unless its German population and the land on which they lived were returned to the Third Reich. The Sudetenland, which had a majority ethnic German population, was a border area lost to Germany at the end of WWI to Czechoslovakia. Danzig, also with an ethnic German population, was part of West Prussia until ceded to Poland by the Treaty of

View of the old synagogue in Aachen after its destruction on Kristallnacht. Stadtarchiv Aachen photo. Courtesy of the United States Holocaust Memorial Museum.

Versailles that ended WWI. Danzig created problems for both the Reich and for Poland. On October 6, 1938, the Polish Ministry of Interior decreed that Poles who had lived outside the country for five years were no longer citizens. Germany responded by dumping 17,000 Jews at the Polish border in early November, many stranded in a town called Zbaszyn. Herschel Grynszpan, whose parents were among the stranded Jews, killed vom Rath in frustration after reading a letter from his parents describing the Nazis' brutality.[8]

Vom Rath's death was all the reason the Nazis needed for Kristallnacht. *They looted, set ablaze, desecrated, or destroyed hundreds of synagogues and thousands of shops. Ninety-two Jews were murdered and thousands were interned at various concentration camps, including* Sachsenhausen-Oranienburg.[9] *"The Nazis wanted the Jews to emigrate so they arrested the men and said to the women, you'll get them back but you have to get out of Germany, in two weeks, three weeks, or a few months," wrote Professor Irene Eber of Hebrew University, Jerusalem.[10]*

Under the Nazi Regime

My mother and father married on June 26, 1938, after their year-long engagement, and lived in Forst-Lausitz with my mother's father, Max. As in so many other cities on *Kristallnacht*, the Nazis ransacked Jewish synagogues, homes and businesses in Forst-Lausitz. On November 10, 1938, the authorities arrested my father and took him to jail. My mother wrote about those frightening days on August 7, 1988. Her words capture the terror of the time:

" " In June of 1938, I got married to my husband
Manfred Oelsner, and we made our home
with my father in his flat on the second floor of a three-story
apartment building. In the evening of November 8, 1938,
Rabbi Cohn and his wife Martha, with whom we were good
friends, joined us as we walked to the house of some mutual
friends.

On the way we overheard some people talking about
bad things which would happen to Jewish people. We were
very concerned and afraid, but continued to the place we had
planned to go. That evening was very strained to say the least.

The next morning my father (Max), who had a route
to deliver different magazines to subscribers, began his usual
routine. He used his bicycle, just as he had done for a few
months already. As it happened, when he came home at noon,
two SA or SS men accosted him in front of our building,
ordered him to put his bicycle into the backyard, and took him
away to the police station. I first heard about this much later
that day.

In the meantime, my husband had been working in a
makeshift home office collecting installment payments from
customers of an already Aryanized business. In mid-morning I opened the front door of our apartment and saw to my
horror, two SS men standing there. I immediately closed the
door and told this to my husband whose answer was, 'When
they have what they want they will leave.'

I think it was only ten minutes later that they knocked on the door, told my husband that he is arrested, and took him away. I remember that I blacked out briefly and when I regained myself I found that they were gone. Our friend Mrs. Cohn tried to stay in contact with the police, and I heard from her that most of the Jewish men in our community, including Rabbi Cohn, were taken to Sachsenhausen *Concentration Camp at Oranienburg, near Berlin."*

My mother was a young woman married only a few months. Without family at that moment with both her husband and father imprisoned, she knew to be afraid of the SS. She would see her husband and father again in January and February of 1939, but alone in November after the arrests, she felt only fear and anxiety.

My father spent two to three days jammed with about 8,000 in a jail room designed for no more than 2,000. They were given a small amount of food and once a day were allowed an hour in the courtyard for air. Two days after being arrested, he and many others were ordered to unload a truck containing sacred objects, including Torahs [the first five books of Moses] and prayer books that they were ordered to burn. Soon after, they were all transported to *Sachsenhausen* concentration camp.

A Miracle in the Midst of Terror

Meanwhile in another part of Germany, the first of major miracles took place that profoundly affected my family. A German-Jewish man named Harri Hoffmann lived with his mother and brother. One evening his ailing mother called him to look out of their apartment window at a flashing orange light.

"Harri, come here. Look out. What is this?" she said.

As they looked, a bullet hit the wooden slat holding the window's panes of glass and then careened off the ceiling and landed on her bed. They were witnesses to *Kristallnacht* happening on the streets right outside their window.

The sky, flashing orange, reflected the fires burning across the city. The bullet that could so easily have killed Harri foreshadowed the near misses he experienced before he was safely out of harm's way. Harri's miracle figured greatly in the miracle of our survival.

The very next day Harri and his brother were rounded up and sent on a train to an unknown destination. Harri's brother, a doctor, approached the man in charge and said, "I have sick people on this train and wherever you are taking us, they will never make it." The guard responded, "Well, get those sick people off this train." His brother walked back and nudged Harri whispering, "Cough like you have TB [tuberculosis]."

Harri's brother got both of them and one other passenger off the train. Since their emigration paperwork was all in order, they contacted friends and relatives in Milwaukee, Wisconsin, letting them know that they desperately needed to leave Germany as soon as possible. After a series of requests, ending with one to Wisconsin Governor Philip LaFollette, they received permission to come to the United States. In Milwaukee, they became friends with my mother's cousins. Later when my parents needed a sponsor to get my family out of Shanghai and into the States, Harri sponsored us. So you see, I would not be here, living this life if instead Harri had been hit by that bullet or murdered in the camps.

What have I done?

Kristallnacht was over but in its wake, my father and grandfather were among thousands imprisoned at *Sachsenhausen*. Located near Berlin, *Sachsenhausen* opened in July 1936. It was used initially for criminals and political prisoners, but quickly became a camp for Jews and others after *Kristallnacht*. Six thousand Jews arrived there in the days just after the pogrom. "It seemed ill-equipped to handle such an influx and was terribly disorganized," my father said. Few supplies of any kind were available and processing of prisoners took as long as twenty-four hours. While waiting, prisoners stood in the cold, waiting, just waiting. My father was lucky because he waited only two hours.

"They took everything we possessed," he said, "and issued receipts."

Some semblance of organization emerged after a few

days. The guards organized work crews into harder and easier assignments. Prisoners walked four to five miles getting to the work sites. Some, like business executives unused to physical labor, failed to accomplish what was demanded of them. The Nazis made it more difficult on them, putting loads of sand into the jacket pockets of some prisoners to make the work even harder. Many died of exhaustion. My father felt grateful that his strength and youth enabled him to do what was demanded of him.

Life was difficult and prisoners were counted like cattle morning, noon, and night. The goal was to make them feel less human. My father witnessed completely burned corpses of those who tried to escape the horror by throwing themselves against the electrified camp fences. One day at a work site, a truck arrived with food for the SS, laden with a stew of lamb and

Inmates at forced labor in the brick works at the Klinker-grossziegel-werke, Sachsenhausen, opposite the main camp which is where my father worked. Courtesy of United States Holocaust Memorial Museum.

green beans. My father asked if they, the prisoners, could have the leftovers. The SS officer said he would let them have it when they were back on the truck and nobody was watching. He was afraid he would get into trouble.

They were given the stew but no utensils for eating it. My father asked about spoons but the officer said that he only had plates so they would have to do with that. With their faces in the plates, the others ate like animals. The officer reproached my father, "What's the matter with you? You asked for the food and now you don't eat." My father explained that he simply could not do it. He could not eat with his face in a plate like an animal.

The SS officer remembered my father, and the next day he approached my dad and said, "Look over there. I'll put sandwiches over there. You eat it because you were so brave yesterday."

"It was a good lunch that day," my father said. The sandwiches of meat and good bread were an unbelievable and very rare treat where starvation was used as a tool for killing as many as possible.

Instances of kindness were quite rare and in general conditions were harsh. Those prisoners with criminal records were often the bosses who enjoyed meting out cruelty to the others. One such cruelty was a "special treatment" given as a punishment for sharing food. Guards filled buckets with ice water and poured it over prisoners.

My father was in *Sachsenhausen* during the winter months and said many suffered greatly. Half developed frostbite as they stood for hours in the bitter cold learning songs for the amusement of the guards or just being punished for some minor "offense." To survive the cold, my father sewed his socks to his long underwear to help keep him warmer. To secure the needles and thread he needed money.

Surprisingly there were canteens in the concentration camps early on. Prisoners could purchase a few extra items, but needed money to do this. When my father arrived, he had only 2 Marks and 40 Pfennigs (about $1.00) on his person and after three or four days, he was out of money. A man who had been in prison and couldn't eat much, gave my father most of his food. This man made cigarettes for himself and extras to sell. When he was released, he gave my father the cigarette maker. My dad then made and sold a few of them to get extra money for the canteen where he bought his needle and thread. "It saved my life," he said.

For Christmas, the guards allowed prisoners to write letters home. My father needed money so he wrote to a wealthy uncle who lived in Berlin. All of his uncle's money and assets

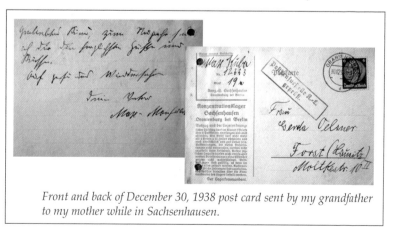

Front and back of December 30, 1938 post card sent by my grandfather to my mother while in Sachsenhausen.

were frozen by the Nazi regime, leaving him to live on a monthly allowance the Nazis granted. His uncle wrote to my grandmother and she, at great hardship to herself, wired 30 Marks ($12.00) to my dad. Wire-transferred money could not be accessed in the camps, however, so my father knew he had to find another way to get some money.

"You have every freedom taken from you. You move from normal life with freedoms to jail and then to a camp with walls," he said. "I asked myself - What have I done? I am not a gangster? Then you find out. You're a Jew and that's the reason. That's the whole crime."

My father's time in the camp was terrifying, and he felt isolated and alone.

My mother received letters from my father, dated November 17th and 20th and January 8th and 19th. With those letters and his oral testimony taken years later, we learned what my dad endured. What he wrote about in those letters showed a marked contrast to what he revealed later because there were specific restrictions regarding what they could communicate. Even so, married only five months, he would not want to frighten his bride more that she already was.

In late January, my father was told he would be released. My father's brother-in-law who lived in Warsaw, Poland, was a friend of the secretary to the Argentinian consul and was able to get a signed document requesting that my father meet with the consul. I don't know if the consul knew what was being signed. I don't know who in fact signed it, but the document assured the officials that my father would be getting out of

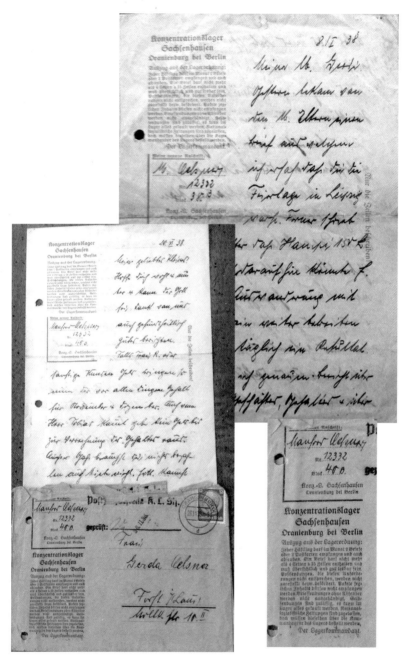

Letters sent by my father to my mother from Sachsenhausen, dated November and December of 1938.

Sachsenhausen. My father used that connection to gain release for my grandfather and others. My father and grandfather were fortunate to escape the fate of their fellow prisoners, most of whom perished in the camp.

Finally on February 7, 1939 at 2:00 p.m., the formalities of release were finished and he was free to leave and go home to my mother and the rest of his family. The 1st lieutenant or *Sturmführer's* parting words served as a warning: "The reach of the Gestapo is going around the whole world and we will be watching you." And true to their promise, the Gestapo's influence ultimately reached Shanghai during the war.

The Nazis gave my father three months to be out of Germany. By May 7, 1939 he had to escape certain danger and find sanctuary somewhere in the world. Until then he had to report weekly to the dreaded Gestapo. The Gestapo or German Secret State Police was responsible for internal Reich security, and "eliminated real and perceived enemies of Nazism."[11]

My father had reason to be frightened.

My father's transition to a more normal life was not easily done. He received his clothes back, now wrinkled and shrunken. Walking around with his head shorn and his short clothes, everyone knew exactly where he had been. He cabled my mother first so she knew he was coming home. Then he contacted his former boss, Dr. Lehman, who gladly offered any assistance. My dad told him about the condition of his clothes so he met my father near the shops and bought him new ones so he no longer felt stigmatized, at least not by his apparel. He couldn't fix my father's shorn head but the clothes helped my father feel more human.

Finally after a train ride of more than three hours, he saw my mother. Bless her heart, she brought him everything he liked: walnuts, cigarettes, grapes. Anything he had ever mentioned to her that he liked, she did her best to have there for him. Together they walked the short distance to home. He requested that she give him the key so he would be in charge again. Inside, friends welcomed him with a huge *weinerschnitzel* [breaded veal], but he found he could eat very little of it. His appetite was gone.

For years he fasted on February 7th, the day he left *Sachsenhausen*, as a way to remember his release. "It is my second birthday," he explained. "I don't know if it's good to remember" he once mused. He gave up the practice on doctor's orders.

His last trip to Leipzig to visit his parents was difficult because they were all frightened about the future. Other family members had been arrested. His mother hugged him tightly and wouldn't let him go when it was time to leave. It was the last time they saw one another.

He began the daunting task of getting out of Germany.

Escape

"They speak almost no Italian. They look Jewish, whatever that means. The boy's only possession is a stamp album. Every week, he shows it to me before we begin our study. Three hundred stamps from all over the world. The Philippines, Bolivia, Tunisia, Algeria, America, Switzerland, Mauritius, Spain, Portugal, Shanghai, Hong Kong, Japan, India, Venezuela, Cuba, the West Indies. I asked him only once, 'How did you amass such a collection?' He answered, 'They're from letters my father received from embassies when we were trying to emigrate from Germany.' The priest looks up and Iacopo asks, 'Can I abandon the boy when the whole world has rejected him?' "

- From A Thread of Grace *a novel by Mary Doria Russell*

"I got released from the concentration camp [and] in three months... I had to get out of Germany. There was only one way out of Germany and this was Shanghai, China. Because you don't need, you didn't need anything [like] immigration papers, [the] only thing you need was ship ticket from Trieste to Shanghai and there you're on your own."

- Manfred Oelsner

Before the beginning of World War II on September 1, 1939, German and Austrian Jews tried desperately to leave Germany and find sanctuary somewhere in the world. The official Nazi policy during this period encouraged emigration. If Jews proved they had the where-

withal to leave, they were free to go but had to relinquish their assets. My parents had nothing the Nazis wanted except their removal from German soil.

The real difficulty lay with the policies of other countries. Few countries allowed Jews to immigrate and only one place permitted entry without a visa: Shanghai, China.

In July 1938, United States President Franklin D. Roosevelt convened thirty-two nations to meet in Evian, France, to discuss the possibility of aiding Jewish refugees to leave Germany. Of those countries in attendance, only one, the Dominican Republic, welcomed Jews to its borders. That said, immigration to other countries, even the United States, was possible, although extremely difficult. America's failure to act after convening the Evian Conference in 1938 set the tone for all future decisions regarding the genocide in Europe. Rescue required commitment and a political price that President Roosevelt was unwilling to pay. He and others, most notably Henry Morgenthau, Jr., Secretary of the Treasury in the Roosevelt administration, wanted to rescue Jews, if only the political fallout were not so great:

'With regard to the political refugees, we are in the midst of the most difficult situation, an almost unmanageable quandary,' wrote Rabbi Stephen Wise, president of the World Jewish Congress to Otto Nathan, one of Roosevelt's Jewish economic advisors. 'On the one hand, the State Department makes all sorts of promises and takes all our lists and then we hear that the consuls do nothing. A few people slip through, but we are afraid, this in the strictest confidence, that the consuls have private instructions from the Department to do nothing, which would be infamous beyond words. What I am afraid lies back of the whole thing is the fear of the Skipper's [Roosevelt] friends in the

State Department that any large admission of radicals to the United States might be used effectively against him in the campaign. Cruel as I may seem, as I have said to you before, his re-election is much more important for everything that is worthwhile and that counts [more] than the admission of a few people, however imminent their peril.'[12]

In the 1932 election, Roosevelt received more than 75% of the Jewish vote. In the 1936 and 1940 elections, he received 90% of the Jewish vote so there seemed little political benefit to aiding Jews for the upcoming 1944 election. In 1944, votes cast by non-Jewish Americans could be lost by fighting a perceived "Jewish" war. In 1944, Roosevelt once again received 90% of the Jewish vote.[13]

The United States State Department was at best indifferent, at worst obstructionist. Breckinridge Long, head of the Special Problems Division of the State Department, was not a bystander but rather an active force for keeping Jews out of the United States. Long used the threat of national security through Nazi infiltration (Nazis posing as Jews) as a ploy to keep quotas from being filled. Applications were onerous: four-feet long, two-sided, six copies needed. Intense scrutiny of candidates as well as of their sponsors was the norm. When Harri Hoffmann's family left for the United States from Germany in March of 1939, his mother, Lena, was only granted a visitor's visa. She left Germany earlier than the rest of the family and was expected to return home because she still had a son living there. Not until Henry Morgenthau, Jr. took his "Report to the Secretary on the Acquiescence of this Government in the Murder of the Jews" to Roosevelt did Long's efforts get thwarted. As a result of Morgenthau's efforts, Roosevelt created the War Refugee Board in 1944.[14]

Escape Routes

For my father the task to obtain passage out of Germany began in earnest. The only place on Earth for them was Shanghai, China, where you could disembark and live with no visa, but he needed boat tickets before they could leave. Border and passport control existed in Shanghai but in name only. None of the governing factions wanted the responsibility for immigration enforcement for reasons of their own.

He needed boat tickets before they could leave so every day he traveled the hundred miles from Forst-Lausitz to Berlin (about the distance from Milwaukee to Chicago), hoping to get tickets. My mother asked him to skip the trip on February 24th, her birthday. He promised he would but then a neighbor pleaded with him to get his sons out of *Sachsenhausen*. He traveled that day and using his connection with the Argentinian consul, he was able to get them freed. The personal sacrifice was my mother's birthday, the first celebrated as a married couple.

My father knew he had very little time to bring about a miracle. After three weeks of searching, his persistence paid off. He had visited the *Hilfsverein fur deutsche Juden* or Aid Association for German Jews looking for three second class tickets to Shanghai. Near the end of April when another family couldn't use their first class tickets, my father was told to prepare his family to go. The agency, however, did not provide money for first class tickets and the agent in charge was rude, wanting to make them feel like beggars. My father's caseworker, a decent and kind man, helped as much as he could. My father returned to the "rude guy's" office and told him it was his duty to help them. He said that was what he was paid to do and time was short. The nice caseworker intervened and within a few minutes the agent approved the tickets. They still had to provide the Italian shipping company, *Lloyd Triestino*, with a guarantee that they would have the money.

On the 2nd of May, my father returned to Berlin and obtained the tickets even though his caseworker had been involved in a motorcycle accident. As required, a customs officer who lived in my parents' building inspected their belongings and approved their removal for the trip as required. They gave notice to the landlord and headed by train to Trieste via Munich, arriving on the 9th of May.

A Respite before the Storm

On May 10th, 1939, they departed on the Italian ship *Conte Verde* operated by *Lloyd Triestino*. On board, they remained frightened but breathed more freely. Though Italy was allied to Germany, my parents felt a growing sense of freedom. They spent twenty-six days on the *Conte Verde.*

"This was the time of my life. We lived in first-class accommodations above the main deck with an air-conditioned room. Whenever we used the towels in the bathroom or had finished all the ice water, they came quickly and replenished both towels and water," my father said.

My parents were unused to such luxuries.

The perfect weather and ideal conditions on the boat made the journey truly pleasant. My parents ate a first-class breakfast every morning of several varieties of meats. "Everything you could think of was there to eat. Life was good," he said.

Many refugees felt as my parents did, wrote David Kranzler in his book *Japanese, Nazis, and Jews: The Jewish Refugee Community of Shanghai, 1938 - 1945*. They appreciated a "relaxed and enjoyable" period of time in such sharp contrast to their time under Nazi terror. Others experienced discrimination and acts of exclusion by a few passengers and even some ship officers.[15] That was not true for my parents who relaxed and to the best of their ability prepared for the days ahead. In anticipation of the tropical climate in Shanghai, they bought white shorts and t-shirts using the 900 German marks [$361.00 in 1938 U.S. dollars] that he had from the *Hilfsverein fur deutsche Juden*.

They wore the shorts and t-shirts for the next ten years while in Shanghai.

The Voyage

When they arrived in Aden, three or four days later, an Italian consul came on board and put new regulations in place for the dinner hour, requiring formal attire. My father spoke with the staff and explained that he did not wish to celebrate in any way as this was not a pleasure trip but rather a journey of incredible uncertainty. My parents wished only for quiet on their way to Shanghai. The headwaiter first suggested he serve them in their cabin but then allowed them to eat in the dining room after the others had finished which perfectly suited my parents.

Once settled, however, they began to enjoy the voyage and the ship's amenities, a swimming pool and a bar on deck. Ninety percent of the passengers were refugees on their way to Shanghai, and none fully understood the life ahead of them.

They spent the evenings on the highest deck singing or enjoying the music with other passengers. They tasted regional specialties from the ports where they stopped. After a few weeks they did not know what to choose to eat as it was all so wonderful. As my father said, "We had a marvelous time on the boat."

Along the way, they stopped at many ports: Trieste, Port Said, the Suez Canal, Aden, Bombay (Mumbai), Colombo (Sri Lanka), Calcutta (Kolkata), Singapore, Hong Kong. For Jewish passengers, access to many of the ports was restricted. When

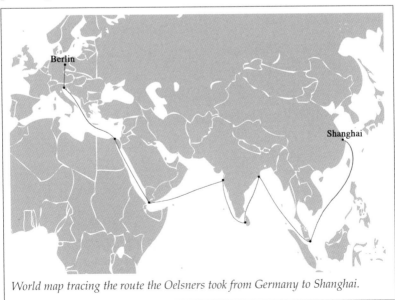

World map tracing the route the Oelsners took from Germany to Shanghai.

confined to the ship, Jewish organizations came aboard to find out what the passengers needed.

They were given permission to go on land in Colombo and Singapore. The first stop at Colombo proved lucrative as my father used his German marks to purchase three cameras, a few bottles of liquor, and English cigarettes from the ship's souvenir shop. He sold each of the cameras for one British pound, which resulted in fifteen American dollars from their sales. He also made a tidy sum on the English cigarettes and tooled leather bags he purchased with the lire he was given in Italy. He told me he never felt so rich in his life. All of this benefited him, Gerda and Max greatly in Shanghai.

At Singapore, my parents were allowed to go ashore, and another miracle occurred in the series that brought my parents safely to Shanghai and then to America. While in a shop, they spoke with the Jewish clerk who had lived in Shanghai. He invited them to dinner at his house and showed them the city of Singapore. The man liked them both and encouraged them to stay in Singapore.

However, the English consulate was closed that day for a religious holiday. Their Singapore host encouraged them to travel on to Shanghai and he would work on getting the papers ready for their return to Singapore.

It was a lucky day for my parents that the English consulate was closed. Soon after the Japanese took Singapore, they forced the Jewish citizens on a death march where they certainly would have perished.

I always tell people that to have survived the Holocaust,

you needed three things: hope, faith, and good fortune. My parents survived because they had their share of miracles. Another stroke of good fortune came the next day. When the ship arrived in Hong Kong, a German man waited at the port. He had lived in Hong Kong for some time and was homesick. He invited the German refugees to a restaurant to enjoy free German food and beer. He even provided transportation to and from the ship. My parents enjoyed a pleasant evening that marked the closing of their journey.

The next day they boarded the ship for the final leg of their voyage to Shanghai.

Their real journey had just begun.

Shanghai

"Shoshona Kahan hated Shanghai from the moment she set foot in it. After only three days in the city, in October 1941, she wrote in her diary, 'What a disgusting city Shanghai is...now I understand why everyone fought with all their might to remain in Japan...Now I understand the terrible letters we received from those who had the misfortune to be sent here. A dirty disgusting city...'"

- Jewish Exiles in Wartime China: Voices from Shanghai, *Irene Eber, ed.*

"Annemarie Pordes... immediately fell in love with Shanghai: 'It was impossible not to love it at first sight...There was the main road with houses built in Western style and right behind it were small Chinese huts, built ...of rough stone, clay, or just bamboo ....They provided living quarters for human beings, their pigs and chickens, all under one roof. What struck me most was the variety of vehicles: trams, buses, cars, carts drawn by water buffalo, bicycles, and in between, weaving in and out, a large number of rickshaws.'"

- Jewish Exiles in Wartime China: Voices from Shanghai, *Irene Eber, ed.*

"In the beginning we didn't have any trouble with the Japanese because they were willing to find cheap labor and this was cheap labor for them.... Still this was very strange, very strange feeling for us because we were Jewish, people mostly...going

through the concentration camps in Germany. We were living in Shanghai, China, Japanese occupied and the Japanese were partners from Germany."

- Manfred Oelsner

Existence in Shanghai was, and is, complicated. In her introduction to *Jewish Exiles in Wartime China*, Irene Eber provides a succinct history of Shanghai's evolution. After the Opium Wars (1839 -1842) the walled city changed. Western powers, most notably the British, established the "so-called treaty system by opening major Chinese cities to foreign trade." The International Settlement and French Concession grew as suburbs to accommodate the new residents. In addition to Westerners, Chinese moved to these areas looking for new opportunities and good living conditions. The British and Americans lived mainly in the International Settlement, the Russians in the French Concession, and the Japanese in Hongkew [sic], once an extension of the International Settlement across the Suzhou Creek.

Baghdadi Jews (Sephardi) came soon after the British and located in the International Settlement. They prospered and had "more wealthy families than any other Jewish community in Shanghai." Russian Jews (Ashkenazi) came in the early 20th century and after the 1917 Russian Revolution. They numbered approximately 7,000 by the 1930s. Much less prosperous and more Orthodox, they were distinctly different from the Baghdadi Jews. Then of course, between 1939 and 1941, more than 18,000 German and Yiddish speaking refugees arrived. "Both a capitalist and cultural center," Shanghai was called the "Paris of the Orient."[16]

The areas were governed by separate councils, which led to fragmented governance at best. Foreign powers possessed extraterritorial rights that gave them the legality to exercise authority beyond their normal boundaries.

Today some 20 million people live in Shanghai, a city far different than the one in 1938 and yet also similar in its poverty. More than 5,000 office and residential skyscrapers form the city's skyline, a number that increases daily. The beautiful Oriental Pearl and Jinmao Towers stand majestically across from Zhongshan Dongyi Road or the Bund, the waterfront on the West Bank of the Huangpu River. Construction cranes create unique patterns in the sky as well. In central Shanghai, luxury hotels abound and modern shopping malls sparkle, offering an array of upscale products, from Gucci to Prada. Open air dining in small precincts is reminiscent of dining in elegant Austrian, Italian, or French cafes. The very wealthy live within the city while the very

Modern Shanghai, September 2008. Mary Murphy photo.

poor live just to the east of the International Settlement in the Hongkou District - home of the Shanghai Ghetto.

Jean Shaoul writes about the level of poverty that still exists in Hongkou in Shanghai: Grinding Poverty Amid Corporate Opulence. *Housing is sub-standard. Families share kitchens if they own one at all. Makeshift kitchens stand in the narrow streets. Modern plumbing is rare and many still use the ancient "honey pot" which must be emptied like the chamber pots of old. Housing prices have soared and real-estate speculation grows making affordable and adequate housing more difficult to find for the working poor. Though the poorer Chinese, who make up most of the residents today, work to beautify the area with common areas where residents stroll, listen to music and practice the ancient art of Tai Chi, the Ghetto itself is threatened with demolition to make way for new profit-driven construction.*[17]

A New Life

On June 4, 1939, my parents and grandfather found a seemingly different city from modern Shanghai; yet the extremes of poverty existed then as they do today. My parents and grandfather were taken to the *Sheffleheim* missionary school, along with forty to fifty other people jammed onto the bed of an open flat-bed truck with sides that rose about eight inches. All were weary. All felt fear and apprehension as they rode through the unfamiliar streets of Shanghai. My father seemed to feel it was an ill omen of not only their future life in Shanghai but of life for all those left behind.

My parents lived in the Refugee-Camp (*Heime*), Chauffoong 680 [sic], located in Hongkou, a poor residential area, best described as a fetid slum. They registered with the authorities, the International Committee for Granting Relief to European Refugees (IC) which was necessary to receive assistance of any kind. Then they were assigned to their temporary living quarters, large barrack-like rooms with over forty-five double beds, closely spaced, separated only with hanging bed sheets giving the illusion of privacy. In fact no privacy existed; no space existed for personal items of any kind. I suppose they put anything they had under the bed for ease of access and use.

The Japanese controlled Shanghai since the 1937 Chinese-Japanese War and were willing to accept most refugees to help build it; consequently, it was not difficult to enter. It was an extremely poor, over-crowded area even before Jewish refugees began to enter. As more and more refugees arrived, there was an increase in rebuilding to meet the urgent need for housing. The Japanese treated them quite well which seemed strange to my family since Japan and Germany were Allies. In July 1942, Josef Albert Meisinger who acted as Gestapo liaison in the area, tried to get the Japanese to exterminate the approximately 18,000 Jews who had escaped from Austria and Germany, thus attempting to fulfill the promise made to my father that the reach of the Gestapo was worldwide. He came with Zyklon-B gas and was ready to build a concentration camp. The Japanese did not agree to his proposals; however, they did build the Ghetto in the Hongkew [sic] area.[18] Rumors spread that gas chambers had been built. My parents heard from some people who said they had seen the chambers with their own eyes. Though no hard evidence exists today, the fear my parents and other refugees experienced was real because they could not disprove the rumors.

Although the conditions were less-than-wonderful, they gratefully received three meals a day provided by the Committee for the Assistance of European Jewish Refugees in Shanghai (CFA), later known as the Speelman Committee.[19]

"For breakfast we received tea in enamel cups and dry bread; for lunch (the main meal) a casserole dish; for dinner tea,

My father and my grandfather, using their two-wheeler cart to transport luggage from the Bund to the Heime or shelters for newly arrived refugees. Oelsner family photo.

dry bread, and two eggs or two bananas" Annie F. Whiting, a Shanghai refugee, elaborated in a 1939 letter written to friends.[20]

My parents remained in the shelter for only a short while and then on March 1, 1940, they moved to 725/83 Tongshan Road, where they shared a single room with three other couples and two bachelors. My grandfather, Max, lived in the refugee camp, the *heime*, the entire time he spent in Shanghai. During the day he worked with my parents at the cigarette shop.

My father and grandfather began figuring out how to "stay above water" and survive financially. Moneymaking opportunities were scarce so they had to be creative. They possessed the entrepreneurial spirit we hear so much about and were not afraid of hard work.

They realized that every few days, boats arrived in the harbor bringing new arrivals. They knew it was difficult to navigate the over-crowded streets so they helped the new arrivals with their luggage, using a handcart my dad had obtained. They received $3 per transport of luggage, so by providing the muscle and working long hours, my father and grandfather made a difference for their survival.

Like so many other arrivals, my father and grandfather, along with my mother, learned how Shanghai business worked. Shops consisted of little one-room stores. Some only lasted a short while and

Bag from our store. Oelsner family photo.

My father standing in front of our 7' x 14' shop on Chusan Road in the Shanghai Ghetto before it was subdivided into living quarters and public shop. My mother and grandfather are standing inside the store. Oelsner family photo.

then just faded away and were simply gone. A Russian bought a large building and turned it into three stores. On December 1, 1939, he gave my father Manfred the corner one for $80.00 a month. My father knew about tobacco from his work in Germany so he opened a cigar and cigarette store, located at 161 Chusan Road.

The middle shop was a Chinese butcher shop and the other one was a barbershop. When the barber didn't pay his rent, the owner threatened to evict him and take his tools. You see, business was very tenuous at best.

By this time, my mother and father had moved into a small room of their own. Knowing thieves were breaking into my father's shop and others, my father wheeled everything back to their room late each night to keep the goods safe. Then at 6:00 the next morning, like clockwork, he carted the goods back to the store.

One day my father said that for whatever reason, he ended up being one hour earlier than usual. "You are like an alarm clock for the neighborhood," neighbors said. Because everyone was used to his punctuality they ended up being early too. He always chuckled about this "funny incident."

Occasionally, he awoke to find a dead Chinese street person outside our door. Residents were responsible for taking care of any dead they found, including funeral expenses, so he dragged any found bodies away from our place. It was another good reason to be an early riser.

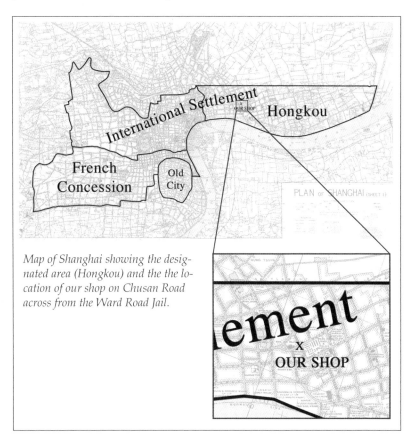

Map of Shanghai showing the designated area (Hongkou) and the the location of our shop on Chusan Road across from the Ward Road Jail.

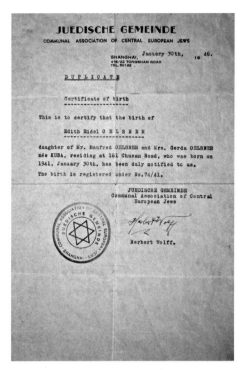

Left: My Shanghai birth certificate.

Below: Both sides of a single telegram sent both ways in 1942. The left side is the announcement from Shanghai of my birth to my paternal grandparents. The right side is the message of congratulations sent back to my parents in Shanghai. It is nothing short of amazing that such messages actually got through in either direction at this time. Oelsner family documents.

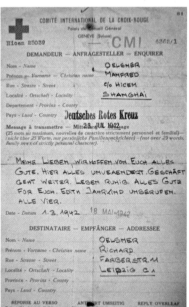

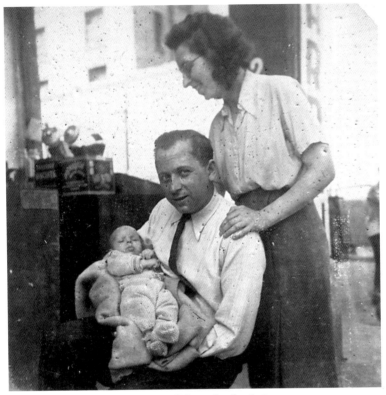

My mother and father holding me. Oelsner family photo.

My Arrival

My mother was alone when she went into labor on January 30, 1941, the day I was born. My daughter-in-law Tzipi said she and my mother talked about that day. My mother walked to the hospital by herself and when she arrived, she climbed a huge flight of stairs. She managed two to three steps and then rested and then climbed two to three more steps and then rested more until she reached the top.

My daughter-in-law imagined how different it was from her own experience giving birth surrounded by so many people who loved her. Her children entered the world in a clean, safe, and welcoming place. My mother, bless her, gave me the gift of life under very different circumstances. Later they sent news of my birth to our family a world away in Germany, via telegram.

Because I was born in China, I was a Chinese citizen who received canned milk from the authorities. For the first year or so, my family sold it for fresh milk. After that year my father had to pay a deposit, a month in advance, to get fresh milk. This was impossible for him to do so he borrowed the money and then of course he had to pay it back.

Our family lived in very poor conditions with no extras. We always needed various items and were very short of money.

A man selling hot water to a woman in Shanghai. Oelsner family photo.

Power was rationed. We used a one-flame cooker or cooked outside on a Hibachi, fueled only with coal dust. Monthly my parents paid $300 in Chinese money for hot water to use for bathing and laundry.

In many ways the poor living conditions made it inevitable that illness would strike. My father had dysentery and ran to the toilet as many as fifty times a day. The toilet was located more than two blocks away. While my dad was ill, a Chinese man stole our all-important teakettle used for boiling water to stave off illness. Mr. Fulhaus, a kind man my parents knew, realized what had happened and came more frequently to buy cigarettes. By selling more cigarettes, my dad earned the cost of a new kettle and enough to pay for his medicine. As soon as my dad was well, Mr. Fulhaus quit coming.

I too became very ill with diarrhea, causing dehydration, a serious concern, especially in a child of only eighteen months. I was very low on fluids and my mother and father had no salt to help with my dehydration. I developed an infection in my right thigh from a salt injection they did manage to get; my mother said that I cried endlessly from the pain. They consulted with Dr. Glass who lived in the French Concession area. He said my dad should get me to a hospital. When they requested a bed for me, the answer was yes; however, when my dad showed them his slip of paper, they refused to admit me and sent us instead to the Jewish hospital.

My father then went to the director of the general hospital in the area, and bartered with anything he owned to pay for my care: shoes, typewriter, an extra suit. He did not have enough money but a neighbor's son needed a blood transfusion and so my dad offered his blood if it would match. Unfortunately, the boy died but afterwards my dad asked the doctor if he needed blood for other transfusions. The doctor quickly responded, "All the time."

"If you help my daughter," my dad replied, "I will give you as much blood as you need." The doctor admitted me into the hospital and after three and a half weeks, I improved and was able to leave. The hospital took care of my physical but not my emotional needs. I returned to my parents as an institutionalized child. My emotions were "out-of-whack" and I no longer cried. I feel such gratitude to my parents for their love, patience and sacrifice, bringing me back to an emotionally healthy child.

The teakettle was not the only item stolen from us. My father told of learning how Shanghai's systems operated. One day my father and a friend were returning by streetcar from the funeral of another friend. They had dressed in suits and hats to honor the seriousness of the occasion.

"The windows were wide open because Shanghai is hot and very humid. At a streetcar stop, a Chinese guy reached in and grabbed my hat. I jumped out and was running and running but there was no sign of the man or my hat," he said. He added, "Stealing isn't against the law in Shanghai. Getting caught makes it a crime."

Another time as my dad sold soft drinks at the shop, a thief stole something from one of his customers. This time he was too fast for the thief and dragged him to the police station. The next day at 10:00 a.m. he and the thief appeared in court.

He recounted in German his version of what had happened and it was translated into Chinese for the judge who promptly sentenced the thief to sixty days.

That was better justice than what occurred with his hat, but he learned soon after, that "justice" in Shanghai had to be purchased. A police sergeant came by the shop and asked if my father had a license for his cart and wanted to see both it and the cart. Dad couldn't find the cart and checked to see if his

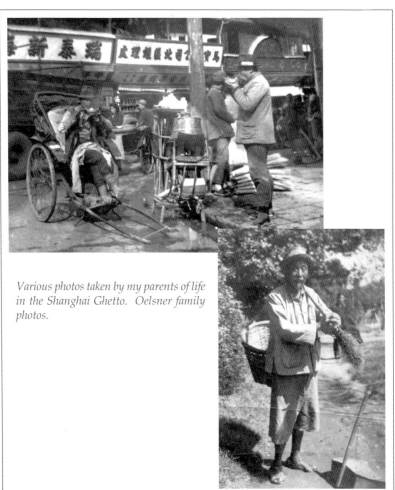

Various photos taken by my parents of life in the Shanghai Ghetto. Oelsner family photos.

neighbor, who sometimes borrowed the cart, was using it.

"No," he told my dad, "not today."

Again my dad was told to go to the police station because the police knew the cart had been stolen. The police had the thief and the cart. Once again he had to appear in court and the translations occurred. Once again the thief was sentenced to sixty days. Then the real bargaining began. The police asked how much the cart was worth.

"Oh, $500? $600? Maybe $1,000." The police responded by asking my dad to pay $500 to get his cart back explaining that it cost money to pay informers to catch thieves and other criminals.

"I don't have $500," my father said. "I have a wife and a child and I need my money to take care of them so keep the cart." The counter offer came quickly. "What would you pay to get the cart back?"

My dad offered $100 and a "take it or leave it" attitude. He got the cart, but he wondered who should get the sixty days, the thief who stole the cart or the police who made him pay to get it back.

He wasn't the only victim of theft. A man he knew was transporting via rickshaw expensive shoe leather to be used in making soles. A thief stole his hat hoping to divert his attention so someone else could steal the valuable leather. Dad's acquaintance kept his attention on the leather and "let the hat go."

Mary Munson Murphy, the writer of this book, told of an episode that occurred in Shanghai not so very long ago when she was traveling there. Their car was making its way through a rather narrow street when suddenly a man on a bicycle fell in front of the vehicle. He lay on the pavement moaning. Another man demanded that they pay for his injuries. Jenny (a Chinese friend of Mary's and her guide on this day) said, "Give him twenty Yuan and that will be the end of it." Their driver did so and the "injured" man got up and rode away. Such was, and still is, life in the Shanghai Ghetto.

From Bad to Worse

On October 5, 1942, my parents partitioned off a small space in the store, living and working there until they traveled to the United States in 1948. The store measured seven feet by fourteen feet. Each partition measured seven feet square. We had no sewer or toilet. Living conditions were harsh. Besides us we lived with rats, roaches and flies. The clothesline that stretched across our living space was black with flies. My father said we were lucky because we only had one fly and the rest were visitors.

My dad wanted to sell drinking water to earn some badly needed money but you needed a sewer, a proper drain, to qualify for the license. My father's ingenuity was amazing. Our place had a cold-water tap and a sink, so he pretended to have a drain connected to a sewer by putting a curtain around the bottom and placing a bucket underneath to catch the water.

The bucket had to be emptied, and emptied often, but he sold water 362 days a year from 6:00 in the morning until

1:30 the following morning. The only days he missed were the High Holy Days of Rosh Hashanah and Yom Kippur.

The borders of that square-mile Ghetto area constrained us, so opportunities for me to explore and grow were rare. I spent most of my first two years in my crib. Sanitary conditions were such that my parents knew I was safer there than on the ground. When I finally could walk about, I was again held to

My father with his signature towel around his neck that he used to keep cool in the heat of Shanghai, pictured with my mother and me. Oelsner family photo.

very strict boundaries. My parents allowed me to do little else but stand in the store. When my father was in the store he had a towel over his shoulder to wipe his brow. When I stood in the store, I put a towel over my shoulder and was proud to be like my dad.

I received a second-hand doll and played with it tirelessly; however, I clearly had dreams of a more elegant doll. I told everyone who would listen, "My grandmother has a big, beautiful doll for me."

I not only had no such doll but I had no grandmother either; still the thought sustained me in some way. My mom, dad, and grandfather heard this "white lie" often and years later when we were finally reunited in Milwaukee, Max, my *Opa* and

my best friend, brought me a big, beautiful doll. She sits in my Fox Point, Wisconsin attic waiting to be restored to her former beauty.

One day, some of us needed to shop for supplies in what we called "the real Shanghai." When my dad concluded his business, we all met and strolled on

Edie with her doll. Oelsner family photo.

My father, my mother and I dressed to go to what we called the "Real Shanghai." Oelsner family photo.

Nanjing Road, a very modern street where five or six huge department stores were located. Dad decided to treat us all to coffee and cocoa. While looking at a table setting in a store window, one of us said, "All the cups have handles." Another one of us said, "Each person has his own spoon." We were duly impressed because it differed greatly from what we lived with every day. When we returned to Hongkou, it seemed even worse by comparison.

Excursions were almost non-existent, but I do remember another one when I was about five years old. I traveled on a rickshaw with my mother. I don't remember where we were going. The coolie who pulled us suddenly let go of the poles, and they flew up into the air causing us to tumble backwards hitting our heads. The excursion was not a huge success, but luckily we were not seriously injured.

Even before America entered the war, conditions in the Restricted Sector were horrendous. In May of 1941, the American Joint Distribution Committee (JDC) sent Laura Margolis, a staff social worker to Shanghai to facilitate re-emigration if possible and to provide relief when not possible. According to Margolis, about 12,000 refugees were living in Hongkou; 8,000 had

Unstanitary conditions in Shanghai. Oelsner family photo.

been certified as "in need of relief." Over 2,000 were still living in the *Heime* or shelters operated for their benefit. In remarks made at the January 15, 1944 Annual Meeting of National Refugee Service (NRS), she described what she found in Shanghai, "...the conditions in Shanghai were such that if it had not been for the work of the Joint Distribution Committee and the fact that the Joint Distribution Committee was able to make credit available to us whereby we could borrow money for these people, half of the population today would not be alive." I have always believed that her tireless efforts saved us.

Once America entered the war, the fighting in the Pacific accelerated and caused further hardships for Ghetto residents. Funds from America dried up. Assets were frozen so the more affluent non-refugee residents who lived outside the Ghetto area were unable to assist. The situation was desperate. Through Margolis' efforts and those of her assistant, Manuel Siegel, credit was established and limited aid was possible. She procured a

Manfred and Max handing out supplies from UNRRA. Oelsner family photo.

more efficient way of preparing food so the relief kitchen was able to serve more meals, although limited funds meant refugees received only one meal a day. By her own admission one of her greatest achievements was to promote the independence of the residents. As they took over responsibility for the community, they planted gardens, organized laundry and mending services and in general worked to make conditions better.

On February 18th, 1943, all Jews had to move to the Restricted Sector for Stateless Refugees, an area of one square mile. Those who had been living in other areas of Shanghai, like the French Concession or the International Area, had to find places to live in the Ghetto. (We already lived there.) The influx of still more refugees into the Ghetto area exacerbated the already horrible conditions.

Allied blockades also caused a shortage of the coal used for cooking and heating. Then the bombing started.

"American fliers based in Okinawa bombed the outskirts of Shanghai where the Japanese had munitions and communications centers," explained my father. "Blackouts were ordered most days and when the alarm sounded, we were in the dark." I was only four years old but I was trained to pick up my water bag and go to the market hall because it had a solid roof. As soon as sirens sounded, I was to go and wait.

Most refugees never worried about the bombing as they felt the Americans would not hit largely civilian targets. "That the Japanese shared this belief is clear from the fact that they stored ammunition in many parts of the Ghetto," wrote Kranzler. Both the refugees and the Japanese were wrong; on

The Hongkou Ward Road Jail and its walls, located across from our shop on Chusan Road. Mary Munson Murphy photo.

July 17, 1945, at 12:13 p.m., the Allies bombed a Hongkou-based Japanese radio station [located in the Ward Road Jail, the prison across from our store] thought to house munitions. Hundreds were killed or injured and whole sections of the Ghetto lay in ruins.[21]

After the War

The war was finally over in August of 1945. People hugged one another, musicians played, and everyone danced in the streets. It is almost impossible to describe the elation that we felt.

After so many dark days and nights, the skies brightened once again and we saw a glimmer of hope. Whatever else was true, most felt that they had survived and could once again begin to live, free in the knowledge that the worst of the danger had passed. In Europe, survivors felt they had escaped some monstrous evil.

Within a few weeks of the war's end, the entire Allied Southeast Fleet arrived in the port of Shanghai bringing with it much-needed food supplies: coffee, butter, meat, canned goods. This show of force was mirrored by "thousands of allied planes that kept coming and coming," according to my dad.

The destruction in Europe began to be fully understood. Life was not easy in the Ghetto in Shanghai, but compared to what we had escaped, we felt very fortunate indeed. Soon we learned the names of the death camps and the startling details about the number of murdered Jews. So many lives lost, so much destruction!

Like other survivors, my parents began the arduous task of trying to put their own lives back in order and to find out what had happened to their dear families. Not all survivors of the Holocaust wanted to come to America. Some immigrated to the newly recognized nation of Israel. Some went to Canada and others tried to rebuild their lives in their former countries.

My parents' hope, however, was to find a way to come to America. One of the first things that had to happen for all of us was a health exam declaring us fit to immigrate. Because my mother had a shadow on her lung, we waited a year until her lung was clear before we could leave Shanghai. I never knew what the problem was with her lung.

Other obstacles were ahead as well. After WWI ended, the number of immigrants who wanted to come to America started to increase. To deal with the high number of immigrants entering the country, the U.S. Congress introduced new immigration policies. After WWII ended, the U.S. government still used the National Origins Quota Act of 1921.[22] This quota limited the number of legal immigrants to 3% of their current ethnic makeup in the United States. The immigration quota system was altered three years later by the Immigration Act of 1924 which lowered the percentage to 2%, severely limiting the opportunities for certain groups to come to America.[23]

After the war ended, while waiting to be allowed to immigrate to the United States, I attended the Shanghai Jewish Youth Association School, located at 627 East Yuhang Road, better known as the Kadoorie School. It was named for Horace Kadoorie who co-chaired the Educational and Cultural Committee for the CFA.

I finished my first year in kindergarten on June 28, 1946. My December 30, 1946 report card indicates I was five years, eleven months old while the average age of the forty students was six years and six months.

"Edith is badly handicapped by [her] long absence therefore her progress during the term was rather slow," my teacher Felisia Larne wrote, but she also noted that my

Dressed to go to school in the few clothes that I had that fit me. Oelsner family photo.

conduct was Excellent." I was ill with whooping cough and other childhood diseases.

According to the report card, I studied dictation, arithmetic, copy writing, art, singing and gymnastics. My only grade of "Excellent" was in gymnastics, but I remember only how much I disliked it.

I spent another term in the Kindergarten Upper

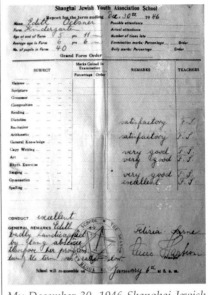

My December 30, 1946 Shanghai Jewish Youth Association School Report Card.

group and then on December 26, 1947, I was promoted to the "Lower School," or what we call lower elementary.

A New Life in America

"I had a brother in **Auschwitz**. *I had my parents in* **Theresien-stadt***. Nobody survived. I had a sister with my brother-in-law and a nephew. They ... were in Warsaw Ghetto and they were fighting there and were killed in Warsaw. I am the last one from my family who survived... We decided we're not willing to go back to Germany. So we decided to go to America."*

- Manfred Oelsner

"I was seven years old and saw grass for the first time. 'Euphoric' best describes my feelings. I rolled on the luxurious grass. Each and every time I saw grass I rolled on it. What a change from the floor of our shop and the streets of the Ghetto!"

- Edith Shafer

A New Home

Finally, we were allowed to come under the United States German quota, but my grandfather was under the United States Polish quota which was more restrictive than the German. Siegbert Altmann, my mother's cousin, filed an application for my parents and me to immigrate to the United States on the fifth of May, 1947. He had to explain that he had the "wherewithal to take care of us."

Harri Hoffman, the same Harri Hoffman who had miraculously survived *Kristallnacht*, sponsored us as well. On January 19, 1948, the U.S. consulate cleared my mother, my father, and me to come to America, granting us certificates

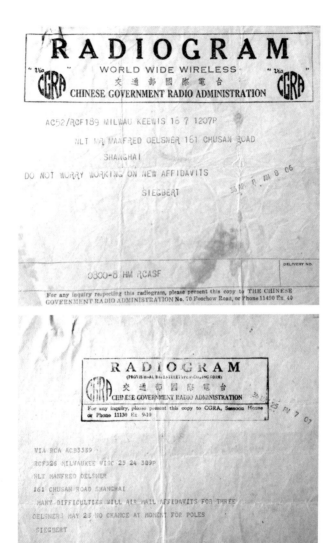

*Two Radiograms sent to my mother, from her cousin Siegbert
who lived in Milwaukee, WI, reporting his progress regarding
permission for us to come to the United States. Oelsner family
documents.*

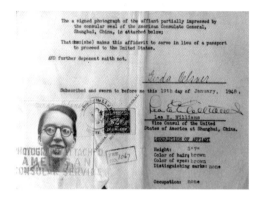

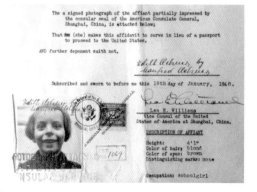

"In Lieu of Passports" documents for my mother, my father and me granted on January 19th of 1948. Oelsner family documents.

"In Lieu of Passports" signed by Lea E. Williams, Vice-consul of the United States at Shanghai, China. We received CNC $3151.00 [Chinese National Currency Yuan] from the American Jewish Joint Distribution Committee - Far Eastern Office for "incidentals."

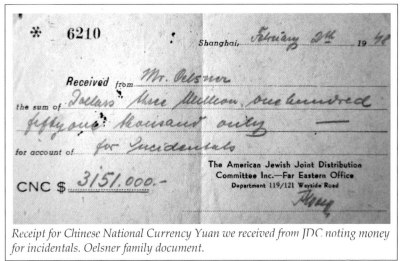

Receipt for Chinese National Currency Yuan we received from JDC noting money for incidentals. Oelsner family document.

Before we left Shanghai, my grandfather, my *Opa*, gave me a delightful birthday gift, a very special book of memories filled with illustrations of life in Shanghai. Although he did not make the illustrations, I treasured the gift as I treasured him.

He had to stay behind in Shanghai. He was born on June 19, 1887, near the Polish German border which became "no-man's" land during the Third Reich. Max fought in WWI and thought of himself as a German citizen, but he too was arrested during *Kristallnacht*. The same Argentinian assistance effected his release on January 20, 1939. Because my grandmother Ida Kuba had died earlier at the age of fifty, he left with my parents, Manfred and Gerda when they sailed for Shanghai.

The letter in the birthday book gift of Shanghai illustrations given to me by my grandfather Max before we left for America in 1948.

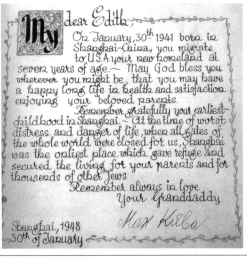

My dear Edith

On January, 30th 1941 born in Shanghai-China, you migrate to U.S.A your new homeland at seven years of age.~ May God bless you wherever you might be, that you may have a happy long life in health and satisfaction enjoying your beloved parents.
Remember gratefully your earliest-childhood in Shanghai ~ At the time of worst distress and danger of life, when all gates of the whole world were closed for us, Shanghai was the onliest place, which gave refuge and secured the living for your parents and for thousands of other Jews
Remember always in love
Your Granddaddy
Max Küba

Shanghai, 1948
30th of January

My grandfather and I in Shanghai. Oelsner family photo.

He had lived in that "no-man's" land zone between Germany and Poland, so was allowed to enter the United States only under the more restrictive Polish quota.

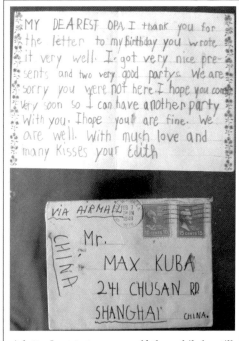

MY DEAREST OPA, I thank you for the letter to my Birthday you wrote it very well. I got very nice presents and two very good partys. We are sorry you were not here. I hope you come very soon so I can have another party with you. I hope you are fine. We are well. With much love and many kisses your Edith

VIA AIRMAIL
CHINA
CHINA
Mr.
MAX KUBA
241 CHUSAN RD
SHANGHAI CHINA.

A letter I wrote to my grandfather while he still resided in Shanghai. Oelsner family documents.

When he was finally allowed to leave and come by ship to San Francisco, the authorities would not let him enter the city. He traveled by train with boarded-up windows to New York City via Chicago. We knew the train was passing through Chicago not far from where we lived in Milwaukee. We were told the windows were boarded over and we would not be able to see him and wave as the train passed by, thus there was no sense in going. The trip to Chicago would not have been easy for us because we had no automobile, so we stayed in Milwaukee and grieved knowing we would not see him on the train.

I felt heavy-hearted and sad as if someone had died because I had so looked forward to seeing him.

When he got to New York, he was shipped back to Germany because of those quotas. He spent time in a camp for displaced persons named *Wildflecken,* a United States-Zone Staging Center. He lived there from November 17, 1950 to January 22, 1951. It required an unbelievable amount of persistence to secure his entry into the United States. My mother Gerda kept remarkable records of their efforts: 44 letters, 2 telegrams, 2 signature sheets, 3 notecards, letters to Wisconsin senators and governors, and even to the President of the United States:

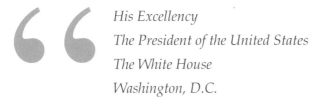

His Excellency
The President of the United States
The White House
Washington, D.C.

Mr. President:

Referring to the Senate vote on D.P. Bill, I would like to call your kind attention to the situation of a group of despaired D.P.'s hopelessly stranded in Shanghai China looking for help and rescue to our great country. Between these unfortunate human beings is my father, Mr. Max Kuba, who was forced to leave Germany in 1939 who has survived Japanese terror during the occupation in Shanghai and has tremendously suffered from inhuman treatments. His only wish now is to be reunited with his children here in the United States, who are the only remaining near relatives after the almost complete extermination of all his loved ones in Nazi Germany. While there are provisions in the present limited D.P. Bill to at least give some relief to displaced persons in

*Europe the suffering group of unfortunate human beings in Shang-
hai China of only 700 persons seemed to be forgotten. We appeal
to you, Mr. President, as the great defender of humanitarian rights
to see to it, that my father's plea could be heard and that our little
family may be reunited and again can live together in peace and
happiness in these United States.*

*Hoping that your good offices may succeed in
this reunion, we are very thankfully yours,*

Mr. and Mrs. Manfred Oelsner

He was finally reunited with our family in Milwaukee
in 1952. He learned English well enough to work at a variety of
jobs, including as a worker in the factory at the now defunct

*My father, my mother, my grandfather and I in a photo taken before leaving
Shanghai. My mother saved this along with so many other documents. Oelsner
family photo.*

T. C. Esser Paint Company, located in an industrial area of the city. We had ten years with him in America before he died in Milwaukee on June 26, 1962, just after his seventy-fifth birthday on June 19th.

The Journey

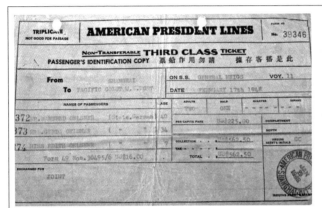

Our American President Lines ticket for passage on the General Meigs that took us from Shanghai to San Francisco in 1948. Oelsner family document.

We left Shanghai in 1948 on the *General Montgomery Meigs*, a ship named for the Quartermaster General who served during and after the Civil War (part of the "Magic Carpet Fleet"). It was a troop transport ship, much less luxurious than the ship that took my parents to Shanghai.

On board we filled out the forms necessary for our arrival in San Francisco. On our way, we stopped in Honolulu where we had a delightful day, "a nice day, a very, very nice day" as my father put it. We were treated to lunch and then given a highlights-bus tour of the island.

I was seven years old and saw grass for the first time.

'Euphoric' best describes my feelings. I rolled on the luxurious grass. Each and every time I saw grass I rolled on it. I delighted in its smell, its color, its texture, its freshness. What a change from the floor of our shop and the streets of the Ghetto!

We reached San Francisco at sunrise and saw the Golden Gate Bridge all aglow. While we were in the immigration line, my parents handed me over the fence to friends who lived in San Francisco. We visited for sixteen days enjoying the company of their friends who welcomed us so warmly and showed us the sights.

My father returned to San Francisco twice more in his life after coming to America and always thought of it fondly as the place he first entered the United States.

We continued on to Milwaukee where we had family. Our relatives, Siegbert, Sylvia, and Lisett Altmann, who were cousins to my mother, knew Harri Hoffmann of Milwaukee, the very same Harri Hoffmann who survived *Kristallnacht* and came to America with his brother and mother. Together they sponsored us. Without the miracle of his survival - that good fortune - we would never have made it to the United States.

We lived with our relatives on Oakland Avenue when we first arrived, but eventually my parents found a small apartment at 14th and Wisconsin, an area that today is occupied by the Marquette University campus.

My father continued to be the "man of the house" just like when he returned from *Sachsenhausen* and wanted to use the key to open the door to their apartment. Although he worked as a laborer in a tannery, he was always proud of the fact that he

My father's United States Certificate of Naturalization granted on February 3, 1954. My mother and I were also granted U.S. citizenship that day.

supported his family. He always managed to do that, even in Shanghai.

When a baseball game was on after work, he sat in "his" chair, his Lazy-Boy, smoked a cigar, perhaps drank a beer and relaxed. The Lazy-Boy was important to my father because it represented his life in his new country. He was so proud to live as an American. We all became citizens on February 3, 1954. After so many hardships and obstacles, we found our new homeland. Our gratitude and pride knew no bounds.

My mother also embraced "America's pastime," especially her team, the Brewers, although she remembered when the Braves were Milwaukee's team. My mom and dad took our boys, Joel and Dan, to their first game at old Milwaukee

County Stadium.

Joel and Dan described their grandfather as a "what you see is what you get" sort of man. He was Joel's personal hero. When he was growing up, Joel never knew the details of my dad's experiences but felt he had "transcended a terrible situation, persevered and succeeded."

Both my sons fondly remembered playing the card game Canasta with their grandfather.

"We were of course treated like children, not as equals," Joel said. Joel learned to play by watching and keeping silent. Both Joel and his brother Dan also remembered Manfred's laugh as something deep and authentic, a "belly laugh." It "rang true," nothing pretentious or false. They always had fun when they stayed overnight with their grandparents in Milwaukee.

He was twelve years old and Dan was ten when my father died. My mother came to live with us that very day in our Racine, Wisconsin home. She was never alone.

Gerda helped with the running of the house and her word with the children was as good as mine. If she said some work had to be done, the boys knew they had to obey. She seemed to want a harmonious existence and enjoyed the peaceful life.

The boys visited my mother while she worked at the Shorewood Village Bakery on Oakland Avenue. It seemed glamorous to them, especially when she gave them cookies. Later, when they questioned her about the job, they learned that it wasn't so glamorous after all.

My sons remembered her singing to them as they were

swinging on the backyard play set. The lyrics were: Swing, swing, back and forth. Because of her accent it sounded more like "Sving, sving, bak unt force." Like Manfred, she laughed deeply and appreciated the gentle joking about her accent.

We adopted our daughter Deborah when she was eighteen months old. She shared a room with my mother until she was three years old.

"She took care of me in every way and was at my beck and call," Deborah said. After we moved to a larger home, "Gram moved across the hall but remained alert to my needs, almost like my own personal night nurse."

Most days my mother and Deborah shared lunches, usually cheese and bread.

"The lunches were delicious and I valued the time with her," remembered Deborah. "Mom and Gram took such good care of us that when I grew older and had a place of my own, I didn't know how to cook and clean because they had taken care of everything."

Tzipi, Joel's wife, had a more mature relationship with my mother. It was to Tzipi she described the difficulty of my birth. A mother herself, my daughter-in-law often thought about how very difficult it must have been.

"Gerda never said anything bad about anyone and seemed to find the joy in everyday things," Tzipi said.

Indeed her delights were simple. She knitted and crocheted for her grandchildren and great grandchildren. Her needlepointed pillows are exquisite. She enjoyed crossword puzzles and playing cards with family and friends. She filled her room with photos of her lost family and though I know she deeply missed my father, she rarely spoke of her grief.

Before she died in 2005 at the age of 91, Danny returned from California. Though she could not speak, she held his hand and said all her good-byes with her eyes. Debbie still longs for time with her. "I sit in my room and cry simply because I want my grandmother." Gerda left a void no one else could fill.

Transitions

Although I have had a beautiful life here, my transition to life in America was not so easy. I spoke very little English having spoken German my first seven years. When I went to school, I didn't understand much and learned by watching. I was placed in kindergarten because I was behind what the other children of my age knew. I was older and taller than all of my classmates.

My parents related a story about my behavior in the school cafeteria. When we were supposed to line up for our lunch, I went to the front of the line. In my mind I was just making sure I would get food, something critical in Shanghai. You did not want to be last in case nothing was left. My behavior, though natural and logical to me, was not acceptable to the school staff. My parents were called in to discuss my bullying of the other students. Today when I speak to students, I tell them about this episode so I can remind them to always treat others with respect. I had to learn that lesson too.

When we first arrived in Milwaukee, we lived with my mother's cousin and his family. Our sponsors thought all our clothes needed to be replaced. They provided new ones. Although they were well-intentioned and acted out of kindness, the effect on me was demeaning and demoralizing. It forced me to see myself as they saw me.

I had been living in our seven-foot square home area in Shanghai and now was able to share my cousin Lisett's room. Lisett was about two years older than I was and used to having her room to herself so she often moved the furniture to change the room. We never moved anything because we had nothing to move so when my bed "went missing" for the first time, I panicked and thought it had disappeared.

Food was also an issue for me. I had survived on watery soup and bread with an occasional paper-thin slice of salami from our neighbor, the butcher. The first time I saw a lamb chop I thought it was shoe leather and practically choked on my introduction to peanut butter.

My parents worked with a social worker to help us get settled and she suggested they send me to summer camp so I would meet children my age. I think Lisett was going to camp so they agreed it might be a good idea. I was seven years old, and spoke only German so I didn't understand what was going on most of the time. The food tasted foreign to me and truthfully, I felt as if I were in a prison.

Years later while recounting my camp experience to a women's group at the Jewish Community Center here in Milwaukee, a woman in the audience said, "I went to camp and I remember a girl from China." I was dumbfounded and didn't know how to respond.

She continued, "I didn't like camp so I went home."

Then I knew how to respond, "I wish I'd known that I could go home too." Even if I had known I could leave, I could not have expressed my wishes.

Eventually, I learned to read and write well in English and excelled in school. I went on to become a teacher, earning a degree in education at the University of Wisconsin - Milwaukee. I taught for only a short time from 1963 - 1964 at Bayside Elementary where I worked as a fourth-grade teacher. Then Neil and I began our family and I quit teaching to raise our children.

In other ways I still struggled to adjust. On September 11, 2001, my family and indeed most Americans were glued to the television, watching the unfolding drama of the terrorist attacks on the World Trade Center and the Pentagon, and of course the aborted attack that ended in Pennsylvania.

Alone, without explaining, I left the house and drove our first car to a gas station, filled the tank and then returned home, took our second car and filled it with gas as well. Then I quickly went to the grocery store and bought everything we needed for the emergency.

I was in survival mode.

Another lingering result of my early living conditions is that I have no sense of smell. None. In Shanghai for seven years, we lived next to an Indian egg dealer. When the eggs fell and broke, they were never cleaned up so we endured the rotten-egg smell that permeated the air. That smell, mixed with the urine smell also in the air, created a lethal mixture that killed my sense of smell.

My father and mother with his parents, his brother and sister-in-law. My grandfather Max stands in the back. The photo was taken before my parents left Germany. Only my mother, my father and grandfather survived the Holocaust. Oelsner family photo.

When WWII ended, my parents, like so many others, struggled to learn about the fates of their loved ones who had remained in Nazi-controlled, war-torn Europe. My paternal grandparents, Richard and Johanna (Schiftan) Oelsner were killed in *Terezin*, also known as *Theresienstadt*. Richard, listed as number XVI/1-305, died May 10, 1943, and was cremated May 11, 1943. Johanna, listed as number XVI/1-306, died May 10, 1943 and was cremated May 11, 1943. Wilhelm, my dad's brother, who was born July 30, 1903, was murdered in *Auschwitz* on March 1, 1944 at 6:50 p.m. His non-Jewish wife, Frieda Ella (nee Franke) survived. Herta, his sister, his brother-in-law Feiwel Gothelf, and their child, Daniel, also known as Wolf, died in the Warsaw Ghetto. Such precise records!

G 1, G 2

Sterbeurkunde

LXVI18/1943

(Standesamt II Auschwitz ——————————— Nr.———)

Der Angestellte Wilhelm Baruch Israel Oelsner —
————————————————— mosaisch —————

wohnhaft Leipzig, Packhofstraße Nr. 1/IV —————

ist am 1.März 1943 ————— um — 18 —Uhr — 50 — Minuten

in Auschwitz, Kasernenstraße ————————— verstorben.

Der Verstorbene war geboren am 30.Juli 1903 —————

in Oppeln ——————————————————

(Standesamt —————————————— Nr.———)

Vater: Richard Israel Oelsner —————————

Mutter: Johanna Sara Oelsner geborene Schiftan —

Der Verstorbene war ~~nicht~~ verheiratet mit Frieda Elle ——
Oelsner geborene Franke —————————

Auschwitz ————, den 22. April ——— 19 44

(Siegel)

Der Standesbeamte
In Vertretung

C 251 ... Sterbeurkunde (mit Elternangabe bezw. ohne Elternangabe).
Verlag für ... wesen G. m. b. H., Berlin SW 61, Gitschiner Straße 109.
Verlag für kommunales Schrifttum und Vordrucke Kurt Gruber, Kattowitz. B-0262

C 251 : C 252

Gebühr RM·60

Documentation detailing the fates of Wilhelm, Richard and Johanna Oelsner.
Ministry of social Welfare Tracing Section Document; HIAS Shanghai document.

MINISTRY OF SOCIAL WELFARE
Tracing Section
PRAHA X., Sadová ul. 12.

Praha on November 2nd, 1948.

No.: C.III/6-8902-8/9-48-11

Obj.: Richard a Johanna OELSNER.

Ref.: Dšk./Sp.

Mr.
Manfred O e l s n e r ,
728 N., 14th Street,
MILWAUKEE 3, Wis.
U.S.A.

With reference to your enquiry we regret we have to give
you the following information that:

No.	Name and surname	Date of birth	Place of birth	Last residence
1.	O E L S N E R Richard	9.1. 1871	-	Leipzig
2.	O E L S N E R Johanna, nee Schiftan	25.4. 1871	-	Leipzig
3.	-	-	-	-

/##/ - were deported to: TEREZÍN (Theresienstadt)

1./ on September 20th, 1942   No of transport: XVI/1 - 305

2./ on September 20th, 1942   " " "   XVI/1 - 306

3./   -   " " "

and from there to:

1./   No of transport:

2./   " " "

3./   " " "

Died:

1./ On the May 10th, 1943   in concentr. camp of TEREZÍN,
was cremated: on May 11th, 1943 - No. 16454,

2./ " " December 10th, 1944 " concentr. camp of TEREZÍN,
was cremated on December 11th, 1944.

3./ " "   -   "   -

H I A S Vertretung   Prague, June 30th, 1948.

H I A S
Shanghai

Subject/ Richard und Johanna Oelsner

Dear Sirs,

With regard to the enclosed inquiry form we wish to inform
your that Mr. Richard Oelsner died in Terezin on the 10th May
1943. Mrs. Johanne Oelsner came to Terezin with her husband,
but is not mentioned in the list of people, who were in Terezin on Jan 1st,1945, It must be presumed, that she died in
Terezin, / as she is not mentioned in any lists of people,
deported from Terezin/ between the year s of 1943-1945, of
which time all records have been destroyed.

Sincerely yours

Signature:

95

Fulfillment

My life in Milwaukee has given me all I ever wanted in life, a family. My wonderful husband, Neil and I met through friends, my girlfriend Alice and Neil's friend Jerry Jacobson. One Saturday night Alice and I went to the Jewish Community Center in Milwaukee for a "singles night."

Alice wasn't keen to go but accommodated my wishes. When we entered the room Alice saw Jerry for the first time and he saw her. The rest as they say is history. Once they were a couple, they tried matchmaking.

Neil played viola for the Racine Symphony, his friend Jerry was in the percussion section. Alice and Jerry introduced us to each other in the living room of Alice's mother. The four of us dined at a place now demolished, but it was located near the current Italian Community Center in Milwaukee. Our first date was not a rousing success. Every time I stood up for anything, he stood up. He loved puns and told lots of jokes. One such joke was "If I could make everybody in America wear a size-12 shoe, that would be no small feat." When I returned home that night, my mother asked me how it went. I told her, "He is a jumping jack, a jokester and I pity the girl who marries him." Within three months, I was that girl.

I knew Neil was the right man for me because he so enjoyed my parents. I had dated before, but those young men were uninterested in even meeting my mother and father. Some were uncomfortable with understanding their conversations because both spoke with German accents.

Neil differed from those men and seemed to delight in getting acquainted with my parents. He dined with us and tremendously enjoyed my mom's beef roast, so much so that my mother's idea of leftovers evaporated.

He also played cards with my father. Two-handed or "Cut Throat" Canasta was one of their favorites. One evening I asked him if he was ready to leave for our date and he replied that we would go as soon as the all-important game was finished. That was when I knew he was Mr. Right.

While out on a date, I said to him, "Starlight, star bright, First star I see tonight, I wish I may, I wish I might, get the wish I wish tonight."

Neil knew my wish and asked me to marry him and I happily said yes. We were engaged.

Neil attended Arizona State College from 1950-55 in Tempe, earning a degree in music. From 1955-59, he played viola with the Air Force Symphony. Neil said it was terrific duty and left a great deal of time for other things. The band arrived at 9:00 in the morning but being a viola player, he practiced at 10:30 in the morning and finished by noon.

He earned his master's degree in music from Catholic University in Washington, D.C. and worked as an elementary instructor in music in Montgomery County, Maryland for three years. In 1962 he moved to Wisconsin and worked for Whitman Publishing in Racine, where he stayed for nineteen years. Though no longer teaching music formally, it remains an important part of his life.

On June 7, 1964, we married and have three children, Joel, Daniel, and Deborah, all blessings. Each is married and their marriages have in turn blessed them with children. We have eight treasured grandchildren. Fortunately most of them live near us so we enjoy them often.

Neil and I with our children and their spouses. Mary Murphy photo.

Our oldest, Joel, a cataloger and his wife Tzipi, a teacher, live near us in Fox Point, a suburb just north of Milwaukee. Shoshanah, Yoni, and Golan are their children. Daniel, an occupational therapist, lives in California with his wife Claire, who works as a sign-language translator, and their two children Sam and Katie. Our daughter Deborah (she prefers Debbie) is a stay-at-home mom to their three children, Rachel, Alex, and Eli and our son-in-law Mike works as an electronic equipment installer. They make their home in Mayville, a town of about 5,000 residents, located near the famous Horicon Marsh, a short hour's drive to visit.

"From the beginning I have felt accepted by the rest of the family. The family structure is strong. I am incredibly fortunate to be a part of it," Mike, Debbie's husband, said.

"Bubbie [Yiddish for grandmother] is my role model and the most important person in my life," Shoshanah told her parents.

That is quite a tribute from my granddaughter.

Giving Testimony

I was seven years old when we eventually left Shanghai. My life differed from the lives of the children I came to know in America, a very foreign place for me. I touched the ground when I was two, saw grass for the first time when I was seven, and had only one toy, a small doll, still a treasured possession. My experiences differed so from my new American friends. I felt different and have felt so my entire life, but none of that matters much in the face of what could have been our fate.

It is fortunate yet difficult to be a survivor; these things, these experiences, these tragic losses of family stay with you. Perhaps that is why I am so grateful for the life I have. Shanghai was the haven that sheltered us from suffering the same fates as our extended families. I don't take anything for granted and show my gratitude for my life in any way I am able.

For many years I never spoke to anyone about my family's experiences. It was too painful. I asked my children to refrain from saying I was born in Shanghai because I did not want to have to explain over and over again. Then in 2008, my daughter-in-law Tzipi, a teacher, asked me to speak about my experiences, saying, "I teach about the Holocaust. I know you're not ready to share your history, but when you are, would you consider speaking to my class?" I said I would.

In preparation, I listened to my father's recorded interview tapes and listed all the important dates. For the first time, before her sixth grade class, I told about my early life in Shanghai and in America. I think I did a horrible job because I focused too much on getting the dates correct, but it was a beginning. Because I felt comfortable with Tzipi, I shared my life's story with her.

Shortly after that, my husband Neil and I visited our son Danny and his family in San Jose, California. Claire, Danny's wife, and I took Sam, my grandson, out for a walk. Claire asked me to tell her about the difficulties involved in adjusting to life in America. As with Tzipi, I felt comfortable and explained just how difficult it had been. She responded with caring and kindness. Her empathy and understanding touched me deeply. I explained how alone I felt at times, how difficult it had been. Her gentle probing freed me to discuss my life. With both Tzipi and Claire, I felt comfortable enough to talk about Shanghai and coming to America.

I began to speak on a regular basis after Arlene Pelz and I became friends after meeting while visiting our loved ones at the Jewish Home and Care Center located on Prospect Avenue in Milwaukee. After my mother died, I continued to volunteer there, doing what were called "friendly visits" to other residents.

Arlene invited me to lunch one day and asked me, "Edie, I know you were not born in America," she said. "There is something in your background about which I am very curious. If you don't want to speak about it, I will understand."

"I was born in China in the Shanghai Ghetto," I replied. "My parents left Germany after *Kristallnacht*."

After my initial reluctance, I asked Arlene "Can I go with you to hear you speak?"

Arlene used to accompany her husband Walter, who had survived the Holocaust, when he spoke about his experiences. After he died, she was encouraged to tell his story.

Arlene was scheduled to speak in Neosho, Wisconsin, a tiny village near Hartford, Wisconsin, located just northwest of Milwaukee. Terry Poland, the teacher, had invited Arlene's husband to speak for many years and it was he who encouraged her to take his place.

I went with Arlene and listened as she spoke to Mr. Poland's seventeen students. After Arlene finished, she asked me to come to the front and introduced me, quietly assuring me that "I was ready."

Indeed I was ready because the next time I spoke, it was to a group of 150 students who attended Jefferson Middle School located in Jefferson, Wisconsin, about sixty-six miles due west of Milwaukee. For the first year, Arlene and I co-presented and after that as Arlene noted, I became more and more confident about speaking in public.

Both my daughters-in-law and my dear friend helped me understand that the whole story was more important than

individual dates. Learning that made my message more power-
ful. Speaking my truth liberated me spiritually. I now say,
"I have been liberated twice. The first was our freedom."

Since 2004 when I first began giving testimony about my
experiences in the Holocaust, I have spoken to thousands of students, adults, and even military personnel. I spoke for *Kristallnacht* commemorations and was invited to be the guest speaker
for *Yom Hashoah*, Holocaust Remembrance Day, in Syracuse,
New York. It has proven to be a most remarkable period of my
life.

Of all my speaking experiences, one is the most memorable. Twelve third and fourth graders, members of the *Shul*
(synagogue) came to our home for a lesson about the Holocaust.
I had asked for the younger children because I felt I could help
them understand the enormity of it, without frightening them.

In my family room, I asked them to sit in a seven-foot-

*I take this suitcase with me when I speak to groups, carrying in it all the
photos and documents I speak about. The suitcase came with me from Shanghai to America and held all my belongings. It measures only 23"x12"x7".
Oelsner family photo.*

square space that replicated our living space in Shanghai. Crowded onto the floor, they had to share the area. They felt the lack of play-space; they felt the confinement. Movement was impossible.

Some years earlier my mother and I taught Neil some German so he could communicate while visiting Germany for work so while we were dining, Neil and I chose to speak in German knowing the children could not understand us.

When questioned, they discussed how difficult it was to feel "out of it." They soon seemed to understand what I had experienced. Their parents told me how much the children learned. The children explained about the difficulty of confinement, of language barriers. Their understanding, their sense of empathy made the whole day one of the most memorable of my life.

I speak when asked because I value the lessons the children and adults learn. More than that I realize there are still some who do not believe that the Holocaust happened. Antisemitic deniers cry loudly that the Holocaust is a myth - a lie. All survivors recount our histories to refute that accusation. We know we will not always be here to tell the truth of what occurred so like others who survived, I embrace the mantra, "Never Forget."

I do my part by speaking about my painful past.

Making sure that all the documents my mother saved so faithfully contribute to the knowledge about the Holocaust is a task I have undertaken but not yet fulfilled. I have contacted several museums including the Illinois Holocaust Museum and

Left: My Bikkur Cholim Award [Care of the Sick] for my volunteer work at the Jewish Home and Care Center.

Below: The minted silver medal received in 2013 from the Spungen Family Foundation at a dinner honoring Shanghai Ghetto survivors.

Education Center located in Skokie, Illinois. Decisions will have to be made, but my hope is that much of the saved material can be useful for various institutions.

I also continue to volunteer at the Jewish Home and Care Center as a Caring Partner. In 2012 [5773], I received the Bikkur Cholim Award [Care of the Sick] for my work as a hospice volunteer.

After I spoke at the Military Post in Grafton, a small town north of Milwaukee, I received a beautiful quilt created by the women there. The quilts are usually reserved for military

personnel as a tribute to their service, but the women who make them felt my "service" as a speaker was valuable and I should have one as well. It hangs in our dining room, a beautiful red, white, and blue tribute. I cherish it.

In Chicago, during the summer of 2013, I was one of a

small group of survivors honored at a dinner sponsored by The Florence and Laurence Spungen Family Foundation. I received a silver piece minted in China as a symbol of the honor. The Foundation gives grants to support health-related issues, especially cancer research, its care and treatment, and to Jewish causes.

The Greatest Miracle of All

Neil and I hosted a celebration for his eightieth birthday on April 21, 2013. Surrounded by family and friends we basked in life's joys. Our three children and their families regaled the gathering with their remake of the song, *We Are the World*. They dressed in everything from alligator costumes to Reggae dreadlocks and belted out their tribute song, *We Are the Children*, to

We celebrated my husband Neil's 80th birthday in June of 2013 with family and friends. Our children and grandchildren sang to their grandfather in honor of his 80th birthday.

Neil and I with all eight granchildren at his 80th birthday celebration.

Neil, their grandfather, their papa.

They sang..."He is the one; we are his children. He is the grandpa, papa noodle, *zayde* we all love. He's turning 80 this year. He does not seem that old. It's true, he makes days great for all of us."

Friends sang along and added, "We're all here today to tell him HAPPY BIRTHDAY. You've seen us through our lives, with laughter, love and joy. We're here to give great thanks and say, you rock!"

As I sat there, surrounded by so many, my thoughts went back to my parents. I reflected on the resourcefulness of my father. He was the "go-to" guy for everyone. He saw solutions; he acted to fix things. In *Sachsenhausen*, it was my father who commandeered extra food for himself and others. In Shanghai, he raised funds for a friend's handicapped child. He worked with my grandfather Max and my mother to distribute food rations. Always he was the man in charge, the man who provided. My mother too was remarkable. She understood the future importance of precious photographs and documents. She managed to save countless letters, pictures and other documents with no air conditioning to help battle the intense heat and humidity of Shanghai. Today those materials serve as a tangible testament to my parents' past, and they provide me with valuable documents to use as I teach about the Holocaust.

So, I rejoice and am grateful for my family and friends, this greatest of all miracles. I would not use the phrase "my life rocks," but I stood in the middle of the celebration and gave thanks for all the years, even the difficult ones. I smiled broadly and laughed, the kind of laughter that makes our face muscles ache, a sweet ache of repeated joy.

Family was all I ever wanted!

End Notes

1   Abraham J. Edelheit and Hershel Edelheit. History of the Holocaust: A Handbook and Dictionary (Boulder, Colorado: Westview Press, Inc., 1944), p. 4.

2   An Interview with Professor Yehuda Bauer, Shoah Resource Center, http://www.yadvashem.org/odot_pdf/microsoft%20-%203856.pdf (Accessed March 17, 2013).

3   Glenn R. Sharfman, "Jewish Emancipation," Encyclopedia of 1848 Revolutions,   ed.   James Chastain.,http://ohio.edu/Chastain/ip/jewemanc.htm (Accessed March 6, 2013).

4   George L. Mosse, German Jews Beyond Judaism (Cincinnati: Hebrew Union College Press, 1985), p. 13).

5   Science as Salvation: Weimar Eugenics, 1919 - 1933, Holocaust Encyclopedia, United States Holocaust Memorial Museum. Holocaust Encyclopedia.   http://www.ushmmm.org/wic/en/article.php?ModuleId=10007062 (Accessed February 17, 2013).

6   Eric Joseph Epstein and Philip Epstein, Dictionary of the Holocaust: Biography, Geography, and Terminology (Westport, CT: Greenwood Press, 1997), p. 33.

7   Ibid., p. 232.

8   Ibid., pps. 116, 350.

9   Ibid., p.165.

10   DVD, Dana Janklowicz-Mann and Amir Mann, Shanghai Ghetto (Rebel Child Productions, 2002).

11   Epstein, Ibid., p.106.

12   Saul Friedlander, The Years of Extermination: Nazi German y and the Jews, 1939-1945 (Harper Collins E-books, EPub Eidition, November 2008) pps. 105-106.

13   Jewish Virtual Library, Jewish Voting Record: U.S. Presidential Elections (1916 - 2012), http://www.jewishvirtuallibrary.org/jsource/US-Israel/jewvote.html (Accessed February 17, 2013).

14   The United States and the Holocaust, Holocaust Encyclopedia, United States Holocaust Memorial Museum, http://www.ushmm.org/wlc/en/article.php?ModuleId=10005182 (Accessed May 13, 2013).

15   David Kranzler, Japanese, Nazis and Jews: The Jewish Refugee Community of Shanghai, 1938 - 1945, (Hoboken, New Jersey: KTAV Publishing House, Inc., 1988), pps. 88 -89).

16   Irene Eber, ed., Jewish Exiles in Wartime China: Voices from Shanghai, (Chicago: University of Chicago Press, 2008), pps. 3 - 7.

17   Jean Shaoul, Shanghai: Grinding Poverty Amid Corporate Opulence, http://www.wsws.org/en/articles/2011/04/shan-a05.html (Accessed January 16, 2013).

18   Patrick E. Tyler, Jews Revisit Shanghai, Grateful Still that it Sheltered Them. New York Times, June 29, 1994, http://www.nytimes.com/1994/06/29/world/jews-revisit-shanghai-grateful-still-that-it-sheltered-them.html (Accessed July 17,2013).

19   Kranzler, Ibid., p. 94.

20   Eber, Ibid., p. 34.

21   Kranzler, Ibid., p. 553.

22   Quota Act of 1921, National Origins Act, http://immigration.laws.com/national-origins-act (Accessed March 17, 2013).

23   Immigration Act of 1924, http://immigration.laws.com/immigration-act-of-1924 (Accessed March 17, 2013).

Acknowledgements

In order to write this book, I needed the help and support of many people and was blessed to receive it.

Nel Brouwer-van den Bergh provided critical assistance. She served as my guide and translator as I tracked down Edie Shafer's birthplace and became my friend in the process.

Stephen Feinberg, friend and former educator for the US Holocaust Memorial Museum provided answers to every question I asked. He shared his knowledge willingly and I am grateful for his assistance. Likewise, other USHMM staff members assisted me with every query providing guidance and knowledge whenever I asked.

Sue Hessel and Gayda Hollnagel gave valuable feedback and technical assistance.

Carl Schulkin and Bill Younglove, friends and colleagues aided me with historical questions, clarifying those "murky" areas difficult to research. Glenn R. Sharfman, of Manchester University gave me critical guidance as well.

Carl Becker and Marcie Hoffman, friends from the Milwaukee Art Museum provided me with research assistance and feedback about the text leading to key revisions.

Rita and Al Hospel generously helped with understanding German language nuances.

I also want to thank Lorraine Hoffmann for giving her time to tell me about her father Harri Hoffmann.

Countless others provided a word, a suggestion, an agency name or a bit of information that proved helpful and to them I am grateful.

Edie Shafer had faith in my ability to bring her family's story to life; for me Manfred, Gerda, and Max are vibrant and alive. I have laughed and cried with them. I thank both Edie and Neil and their children for giving me that opportunity.

Finally, I want to thank two very special people, my husband and my daughter. Sara worked with me on the book and she too grew to love Edie's family. My husband Terry has given me all the love and support any wife could ask for and I could not have written this book without him.

Mary Munson Murphy

When I began working on Edie Shafer's memoir I naively thought I would walk away from this project feeling that I would give as good as I would get. The truth is that I am the one who was given so much more. Edie Shafer has reminded me to be grateful, to take time with your family, to give back. She has shown me that even in the face of such adversity, with love and hope we can persevere. As well as this, she has shared her story, the story of her parents, and with it the story of so many others, the Shanghai Jews. I am honored and completely humbled to have worked on this book. Edie Shafer is the final miracle in her family's story as she is a testament to all that they unwaveringly fought for.

I would also like to thank my mother, Mary Murphy and my husband, Nathan for making this project possible.

Sara Sillars

I

Transcription of 1967 Interview with Manfred
Oelsner conducted by his son-in-law Neil Shafer

The following is a transcription of the July 1967 interview conducted by Neil Shafer with his father-in-law Manfred Oelsner. The interview discusses Manfred and Gerda Oelsner's emigration from Germany, their immigration into Shanghai, their life in the Shanghai Ghetto with their daughter Edie Shafer, who was born there, and their eventual journey to the United States after their liberation when World War II ended.

It is important to note that Manfred Oelsner was a German refugee and therefore English was not his native language. This transcription has been completed as faithfully as possible; however, when clarification became necessary, those notes were put in brackets [].

Disc 1

Neil: This is the start of the first recording about the years in Germany that Gerda and Fred spent before the war and then the story of what happened during and after the war throughout, the eh, those years. I think that we can just start by talking about how you felt when the Nazis came to power. This is the first thing.

Manfred: Now in the beginning we were a little bit scared. Uh, we didn't know. We were knowing it was coming something up against us. We weren't able to figure out how much so and how much running and how much fighting this would take to come over the time. We were scared obviously. We were waiting what was coming up.

Neil: Why were you scared? What scared you?

Manfred: The Nazis when they were taking over in January after the election, they were sending the SR boys, 17, 18, 19 year old boys in the streets with guns. The way they were putting it to keep order, and it, it was quite an unusual situation.

Gerda: I must admit it was an unusual situation but I don't think we were so scared [as they were] in the big city where it was different from our small space. We think that the whole situation would blow over very fast. Our merchants could still keep their stores, at least in the beginning, and we heard only from the very rich people that they left the country and tried to go to America, Australia or so.

Neil: Most of the Jews in Germany stayed there because they didn't believe what was going to happen. Isn't that right?

Gerda: Ja.

Neil: You were hoping it would blow over. (**Gerda**: Ja.) Hoping things would die down as you figure they might normally in any sane situation. Any situation that was a logical thing to assume that such recklessness would never come to power. (**Gerda**: Uh-huh.)

Gerda: Hitler had written that book *Mein Kampf* but I don't think we believed, we didn't believe it would be possible for him to do the things he mentioned in that book.

Manfred: In the beginning I was quite close to the situation and I still, I don't know, I don't know, because friends of mine, I was a bowler in Germany, friends of mine, they were Nazis and they knew I was a Jew and they were coming and telling me, Hitler is taking everything from the Jews, sending them to concentration camps, killing the Jews. He is taking good care of the Jews. We weren't believing, I mean something was coming up. Otherwise there was plenty of organized labor. They were against Hitler in the beginning. However he was tying everything down. He was bringing up a situation where one was scared of the other, of the next one, of his best friend. No one was willing to talk anymore. No one was willing to do anything because he didn't know the proper feelings. He didn't know the proper way of what the next guy was doing to him. So, everybody was tied down.

Gerda: Hitler called the things he undertook against the Jews he called those actions; I think I remember that right. There was something going on in Breslau again in a larger city.

Neil: What year? You talk about? This is still the early part of '34?

Gerda: '34 or '35. There he even put, lawyers and doctors tried to convert to Christianity and they thought they would be rescued by that. But he put them into jails and in a small town we believed that again it could only happen in a big city.

Neil: But that happened in a small town too?

Gerda: No, not in our place really. No, not at that time.

Neil: But all of this created a feeling of ill...

Gerda: It was an uneasy feeling. But I think, we in our eastern part of Germany we hardly knew what an American consulate is. But we had a friend and he came from the western part of Germany. He was a clerk in one of our Jewish stores and on one of his vacations he went home to the western part of Germany and there he didn't come back from that vacation because they had it very easy. He went to the consulate, applied for the visa, got it and left. It was in two weeks or three weeks at that time, he had gone out of the country. We still thought these were only special cases, only a few, and gosh we were so German that we did not think it could happen to us.

Neil: I just want a general feeling of how it was. And um, things got worse and worse through the years, is that right? What happened to make it get so bad?

Manfred: Step to step, first time when Hitler took over he was very busy with his own problems. Because first time he was willing to reorganize the whole country. For the way and for things he was willing to do. So first time he was looking for work for the people. Everybody knows which way. Then he was taking that island back. Then he was taking Czechoslovakia and then he was taking Poland.

Neil: Well that's foreign policy. That's...okay. What happened to the people that made it bad and worse and worse until you were taken and out of the country?

Manfred: Let's put it this way, everybody who was in opposition to Hitler, and people they were in strong positions with his opposition. He took them all in the beginning was taking them into concentration camps. They had concentration camps ready and they put them there. This was half a secret matter. This wasn't so openly about concentration camps were there and he took them in. So, he was breaking the power of the opposition, first completely. He took command, Communists and the Democrats. He took them first. Then by and by he was strengthening the position.

The normal German people in their scareness they were willing to donate to the Nazi party. They were willing to get the members. And so Hitler was not only coming into real power, he was coming into money. He was building up so by and by he was stepping up. Ja, I was one of the earliest who lost their job because I had a tobacco store in a big bowling place from the organization and all of the members were coming there and Hitler took over and three weeks later I lost my job. Because everybody had to apply for membership in the workers organization from the party from the NSDAP, Nazi Party. Then I was drifting around looking from one job to another job.

Neil: What did you do? How did you survive then after you lost your job?

Manfred: Part time work.

Neil: Who hired you?

Manfred: After that I was a salesman for vacuum cleaners.

Neil: A Jewish firm?

Manfred: A Jewish firm, yes. We were going out and in the small cities and towns and were coming in, "Heil Hitler", selling.

Neil: So the first thing that Hitler did was to make the Jews work for Jewish firms if they wanted jobs. Really that's what it amounted to. He took all the Jews out of other jobs. It wasn't a written policy but that's was effectively that's what it amounted to...

(Everyone talking together)

Manfred: He was looking for people that were able to take over the Jewish businesses. They were giving him very cheap money offers and then they were throwing you out and taking over the business. Nobody was able to get that money anyhow because it was going into the bank. It was locked right away. You couldn't do anything with that money and they were giving you a special amount of money for cost of living every week out of your account. All the money was frozen. You were willing to have some money then you had to apply for it and like a beggar to beg for your own money. Then...

Neil: That was the money that the Jewish firm owners had for their firms. So you had a job as a vacuum cleaner salesman and you quit that?

Manfred: That firm was liquidated. Then I was working in a Jewish restaurant as a houseboy. I was cleaning up the trays as a busboy. There I was working there till the whole thing was broken down for one and a half years until 1937. I was going to Forst-Lausitz. There I was working at a credit store. I was working as a delivery boy for a Jewish firm, working my way up. I was going to court. I was writing the suits in court. I was going to court and this time I had a really uneasy feeling because the judge there he was a Nazi too so you have to fight for the money of your boss and there's a Nazi there and so that credit business in Germany it was same like cutting somebody's throat.

Neil: What year was it that you actually lost your first job?

Manfred: '33

Neil: You lost the job in '33 and then you worked as a salesman until?

Manfred: 'Til '35 or '36

Neil: Two or three years and then you saw things getting worse and worse?

Manfred: I couldn't, we couldn't run because we were always one step away from a concentration camp because there was suicides from house to house...

Neil: You didn't know what would happen.

Manfred: No, we have to come in, we had to greet everybody with "Heil Hitler" otherwise you weren't willing to make a business. So if one doesn't have their papers or if someone is getting suspicious he is willing to check on you and you are coming in with Heil Hitler and you are a Jew and you are obviously going to a concentration camp.

Neil: Is that right?

Manfred: Sure. Then my last job in Leipzig was in a clubhouse from the Nazis.

Neil: This was after a busboy?

Manfred: Before the busboy. '33 I was getting fired in the bowling alley. Then I took a job in Kaizer and it was all the SS people a clubhouse it was the second job in the Nazi house and selling cigarettes and shopping for kitchen and so my boss was a very, very nice guy.

Neil: And your boss knew you were Jewish?

Manfred: He knew this and we and the doorman there and he was a very old member from the party there and he was digging into my feelings and he was finding out that I'm a Jew and one day he approached me and said,

"Listen, what are you doing here?" and I said, "I'm working. I'm making a living." And he said, "No listen you are a Jew you don't have anything to do here. Are you spying?" I said, "I'm not spying. I have to somehow make a living."

And he accepted me because during that year before he was starting to dig in we were getting friends and I knew he was a Nazi, what should I do, you somehow you had somehow to make a living. Then they were coming from the Nazi party and they were willing to organize their labor too and they did it up because they knew up there and then everybody was shaking and everybody had to have their work papers, hours books. They were coming and saying,

"Do you have one?"

"No"

"Why not?"

"You know I am a Jew"

"You are a Jew? You are fired."

"You can't fire me. The only person who is able to fire me here, is Mr. Abel, he is the boss. When he throws me out then it's ok."

Now in this one and half years I made very good friends with the Nazis and they knew I was Jew and they knew it too. There was a guy who was a *Haupsturmführer*, three stars and he was an accountant and he was traveling around Germany and he was making orders in the books with money and he got quite a party job, you know? And when the trouble was coming I went to him and said, "Say listen, this happened and what should I do, they are willing to fire me?" He said, "You stay here. You go up tomorrow in the main office and you tell them I am sending you and I am after tomorrow and next week I am in Berlin anyhow so I will bring you permission papers that you are able to work here. And tell them they have to wait until I am back." Okay I was going up the next morning and I told them what happened and they said all right they would wait until he gets back.

He was away for three weeks and after three weeks he was coming. We were open longer hours Friday evening and Saturday evening. Normal business hours we were open until one o'clock and this two nights we had open until three o'clock and he was coming in about ten minutes until three on Saturday night, just from the trip first thing he was coming in. Everybody "Hello. Hello. Hello". He was leaving everybody standing and he was coming to me where I was standing. He said, "Fred, you don't have to worry about anything. Here are your working papers."

So now I was working there with permission and it was going on 1936 vacation time. I was willing to go to make a trip to the Baltic Sea and we did it. My boss told me, "Don't do it. Don't go away. When you are out for fourteen days I'm not able to hold you any more." I said, "I don't care. I need a rest." I'm going to the Baltic and when I came back…no more job. I will never forget how nice and kind Mr. Abel was to me. The last day when I was coming in and he told me I'm not able to work anymore he told me, "Fred you should know one thing, when the situation is coming up that you are very much in trouble you have always one table where you have something to eat and you have always a house where you are able to find a home. With trouble or without trouble, if something comes up you can count on me."

Neil: We will now continue with the second session.

Manfred: From there first I was somehow to make a living, father …..my brother he got killed in *Auschwitz*, he was selling vacuum cleaners as a salesman, so I was looking for a license and I was going along. In the beginning this was a very hard time and then I picked up and I was going along. This wasn't going for a very long time and the Nazis were cleaning up this business too and I was jobless again. This was maybe a job for three or four months. Then there was a Jewish eating place in Leipzig then I was starting there as a busboy. House boy and bus boy and this was a job for about another four or five months and then one of the three brothers in the meat shop and eating place, one of the three brothers – he was willing to leave Germany with lots of money was willing to go to Czechoslovakia and they catched him at the border and then they closed that business too.

And then in the beginning 1936 Christmas I went where my fiancée lived for a visit because I had an aunt in the same town and there I got an offer to work at the credit store beginning at the houseboy too, delivery boy and general helper. And then in the middle of January of 1937, I moved to Forst-Lausitz, where my fiancée lived and from there I was working with this company Carl Horn Nachfolger. My boss she was a widow. She was working on immigration to South America and she was showing me everything and so by and by I was the salesman. I was keeping all the books there and I was going to court to fight for payments from the customers and it was a very dangerous job because the judge himself, he was a Nazi and he knew I was a Jew and sometimes he has to give me court orders he wasn't willing to give me. The situation was in my favor and the management in Berlin and the credit store was six or eight branches and my management was willing to stick their neck out. Then in June of 1938 I got married and in view of, it was a company-quite a job and I was getting married.

Neil: How long were you engaged?

Manfred: We were engaged about five or six months. We knew after six years the day, the date and the hour we were standing under the *Chuppah* when we first met exactly after six years. And then we got married and right away after we have to liquidate our store because the owner was giving us notice that we have to leave there and then my boss was coming and he didn't know what to do and from which point else he should liquidate the store. This was about twenty-five miles away from Forst-Lausitz, we had another store and Mr. Tobias was store manager there and he was taking over quite a bit of the merchandise and all the books. I told my boss, Mr. Neiman, we can take in my home and I am willing to liquidate that store from my house. And so we did. The whole outfit was in my house for about three or four weeks.

One day Mr. Neiman and Mr. Tobias, they were coming and they were willing to tell me they are paying me too much wages. I'm just married and I was depending on my income that I had. They were willing to tell me that my wages were too high and the company wasn't able to afford, at that time the Jewish people they weren't able to pay so much. They were losing thousands and thousands of dollars and my wage was about 350 *Marks* in months and so I told him and I am in this case very short and very strict, so I told him, "Dr. Neiman, in case you are not willing to go along with the arrangements that we had, okay there is the door. And by the way take the books, take everything out of here and leave me alone. Take the safe." They brought the safe in and everything. "Take the books and take the safe." Then my late father-in-law he was very excited and my wife was very excited and they were taking me outside and we had a conference and we had to talk and I shouldn't be so rough and we didn't know from what we were able to make a living the day after tomorrow so I told them leave it to me, they are not able to throw me out because they need me, they don't have anybody who is able to liquidate that store in that little town. So I was stiff and I was standing at my demands and I won and this was the way I was willing to have it. This was in August 1938. Early November 1938, now it's coming a very dark chapter of the story.

Saturday mornings when I was going out, we were married; we were willing to live a little bit. This was Monday morning. Usually Saturday morning when I was going out to visit some customers and to cash in some money I was coming back and I brought along hot hotdogs and then we were sitting down and we had a little brunch and early in November in Paris, one Polish guy Grynszpan shot a German consulate [sic], he shot him. The Germans had taken Grynszpan's family and put them all in concentration camps and killed them and he was so mad at the Germans that he took that guy and shot him and so he was very critical condition for a couple days.

Neil: Now wait a minute, before this shooting the Nazis had taken his family already and killed them?

Manfred: Ja, ja, sure in Poland. This was on a Thursday or Friday that this guy got shot. Saturday evening we went to a birthday party at a friend's house he got the hardware store. We were sitting up there listening to the radio and everybody was scared. The rabbi was there and we celebrated the birthday and we were playing cards. Everybody then went home and it was looking very black in the future what was coming up. (*Gerda corrects*) The next morning I went out and when I was coming home with the hotdogs. My wife was very excited she told me there was two SS men standing before the door and were watching who was going in and who was coming out and she said to me. I said to her, "After they have us they will go away." And they did.

After they took me along they were going away with me. They were taking me to the police station and the city jail like a gangster who did the worse things in his life. I had to have my hands behind my head, behind my neck and they were going behind me throwing guns and they were putting me in that jail. In the jail... All the Jewish people that were living in that little town, they were there. We were all in one small room, two small rooms, capacity of usually one or two thousand and we were eight to ten thousand in one room. We got little bit to eat, not much. We got one hour a day in the morning. Morning and noon half an hour to get air. We got a chance to walk around outside in the backyard in the courtyard and then we have to go back to our cells. A few hours later my late father-in-law was coming too and so we were staying in jail for three or four days.

On the second day they brought all of the religious books, all the Torahs from our temple. They put it in the market place. They brought it in trucks. All the Jewish prisoners had to come out and had to unload the trucks and put everything in a big pile and then they put fire to it and they burned it.

And the next day they ordered the big truck and from there we were loaded into the truck and then we were going to Berlin to the concentration camp *Sachsenhausen*. Then a bus trip for six or seven hours. We left early in the morning. We arrived early in the afternoon. There was the concentration camp. People over people were standing outside because they were coming from every spot in Germany and the whole arrangements weren't really organized enough to take so many people in so short a time. There were groups that were standing 24 hours before they were able to find the luck to come in and to live through that terrible experience, ordeal of what was ahead of us. I was more of the luckier groups. We were standing out only for one and a half or two hours. Then they were taking all of our belongings, making notes what we were leaving there receipts and then they put us in the big bathroom, we got our showers, we got our haircut and our concentration camp outfit.

Neil: Haircut and they shaved your head?

Manfred: Shaved our heads, yes we didn't have any hair at all. And then we got the pair of pants and old army jacket from the First World War. Fitting or not fitting, one guy had bigger stomach so whole thing out, and then no hair, one guy had biggest at all. Then we were coming in the barracks and there was nothing. There was nothing ready in the barracks. We were sleeping the first eight or ten nights on straw. There were no dishes, no forks, no spoons, nothing.

The number one guy he was an elderly inmate from a concentration camp. They called it the BE [*Berufsarbeiter*] – official criminal, people with a very long criminal record and this was our boss there. In the beginning he was looking for a few guys who were willing to give him a hand and to organize the whole thing so I was sticking my neck out too and we had to go in the big kitchen to get all of our utensils, plates and forks and this stuff. So he was showing us around the concentration camp and the first thing that I saw in those first few hours there was the electric fence and two bodies hanging in there completely burned. They were willing to escape out of that camp and they weren't believing in the power of the electricity and they paid for it. So no toilets, nothing in that barrack. So then, we got our dishes after waiting three or four hours we brought in our dishes and we were starting to get organized.

Then after we were in there for two or three days we have to report for work. There were easy assignments and harder assignments. There was a *klinker*, work where they were building an airplane field and airplane factory and a waterway from the airplane factory to the Kaiser Wilhem Canal, water channel. I was going out to the *klinker* [brick factory] and there we had railroad tracks and railroad cars, shoved full with *Zent*, with no engine to it. Iron wires before the railroad cars. Twenty guys in front and wires over the shoulders when the cars were filled, we had to move it out. The SS were behind us and the guys were hitting the men with whips and they were scaring the people with guns.

There were different places to work. There was another group they had little trucks and they were loaded with stuff that was coming by boat from one side and they had to bring it in the building, stones and cement and all the things they need for building. There was another group; they had to carry stones on their shoulders up to the place where they were building houses for them.

Then there were groups that were unable to get a job because you have to look that up every group of human body was together. People from every walks of life, executives and businessmen and laborers. One group was able to work do physical labor another group wasn't able because they weren't used to it. And they were expected from everybody hard labor. (*Clears throat*)

A group of a few people were in that camp and they hadn't, had proved they weren't able to work and they were giving them smaller assignments. Let's say they had the military jackets the army jackets with three or four buttons in front and back closed. They were turning the jacket around, close the jacket in back and then you had to lift up the ends and then they were putting in cement, plain cement, and they were sending him forever mile with that cement in front of his body, he has to leave it out there running and then he has to run it back and they fill it up again and he was bringing that cement again. There was no productive work at all. No reason for all for that. Not only to occupy him, just opposite to kill him automatically.

Neil: Wear him out.

Manfred: Wear him out. That's it. So, I feel myself I should say I was very lucky in the concentration camp because there was in bloom of my power because I was just willing to start life so there wasn't anything was able to be too black for me. I was always looking, looking a little bit with everything up from the sun side so I was waiting for tomorrow and after tomorrow the whole thing was over. And then very terrible thing was that marching from and to the camp because this was laying outside about 4 or 5 miles out of the concentration camp and we had to walk, I was up there in the morning and in the evening we had to walk back. Surrounded by SS people when the march was starting, surrounded first time everybody was, his number, his concentration camp number was marked down. Then they were counted like cows they were going to the slaughter market, to the slaughter in Chicago. It's a meat market. Then you were starting, everybody was starting to work, at noon we had a half an hour lunch. Everybody was bringing out what they had to eat we have to stand and we are eating and there is counting going on. Then after they found out everybody was there then we were able to get 15 minutes time for eating and then you had to go to work again.

I never will forget...I think I have to give a little bit for explanation. I was never used to have bigger amounts of money on myself so when I was in during the concentration camp I had two *Marks* and 40 *Pfennig*, German money in my belongings. You got the chance to buy something. They had the canteen. After three or four days, I was out of my money. So, I had to do some organizing so there I met a guy, he was coming from the *Zuchthaus* [penitentiary].

Neil: What's that?

Gerda: Penitentiary.

Manfred: The penitentiary. He was three or four years and then they, and then he was coming to the concentration camp. He wasn't willing, he was able to eat anymore much and first thing he was sharing his ration bread with me. I was able to eat three and a half or four pounds of *Schwartzbrot*, three or four loaves of bread. I was able to eat and I didn't have it because there was no food, and hard labor.

So he got a little bit a machine, two rollers and a little bit of cotton going between the two rollers and there you were able to make cigarettes. And after I was there for a week or two, they were sending him home. And then he was giving the give-away present to me, this cigarette machine. And this cigarette machine, I should say, that saved my life from concentration camp. Because everybody was buying tobacco, this was much cheaper cigarette tobacco and I was sitting in the evening and I was rolling cigarettes and each packet fifty grams, fifty grams of cigarettes, fifty grams of tobacco you got out forty-five to forty-six cigarettes and there I made three-four cigarettes for myself and I was obviously a smoker so I had enough cigarettes.

And one day, now let's come back, this was a little bit in explanation, now let's come back to the brickyard and to the commanders there. One day it was the middle March, 1939, I was there already for, no this was in the beginning of...ending of January. It was the 7th of February I was going home. The beginning of January they were willing to send out [a] commando and work, group of workers to find out the head, at about three and a half or four miles from that *klinkerwagon*, they got that, now this is very hard to explain in English ...lame, eh, ja, ground, ja ground was clay so same so let's say ground like the desert, and this was a little bit wet and working with that and using that clay to build stones together and they were willing to send six or eight people out to find out they were able to take some clay out of there already.

And then the one guy he was in this commando he was coming was going through the prisoners and was asking every-

body, "You have enough cigarettes?" "You have enough cigarettes?" "Ja why?" Well then you can come along. I promise
you we have a nice and pleasant day because we are going out
to the *Lehm Grube* [clay ditch], that's what the name in German
is for that we were going out in the *Lehm Grube*. We have a
nice day. All right just this day I had enough cigarettes because
the day before I was making out, I was making cigarettes out
of fifteen, I guess fifteen packages of tobacco. So I had about
fifty cigarettes which was plenty. And I was going along. So
we were coming out with that army truck and the highways in
Germany were *Kopfpflaster*. This was stone by stone, was stone
by stone not same like here in America, asphalt?

Neil and Gerda in unison: Cobblestone!

Manfred: Cobblestone! And this was a very, eh, uneasy ride,
in that eh,

Neil: Bumpy.

Manfred: Bumpy. Very bumpy, ja. So we were going out and
then we had three SS, four SS guys there to watch for us. We
were seven or eight people out there. And we got stuck with
our trucks and we were willing to pull it out. The way I
learned it later, at noon in the camp they were counting the
prisoners at noon and six guys were missing. And the alarm
was going and everybody eh, was excited. Six guys they escaped so somebody was coming and "Oh, we sending a group
up there in the *Lehm Grube*."

And then they were coming up with three big trucks, three big
trucks and they found us there and they brought two big con-
tainers with food for the four SS guys. And I never will forget
this was the *Hammel Fliesch* [lamb=mutton] between the bone.
Green beans and lamb, lamb meat. And a little bit so like stew,
not too, not too heavy, so same like a soup. And the guys were
eating and we hadn't got anything to eat yet. We were hungry.
We were hungry alright. And then we were together and then

the question was coming up. Who got the nerve to ask the SS
men for a little something to eat? Because we were hungry. So
I have to, got guts. So okay I asked them. And he said okay, I
am willing to give it to you. Our first time not here. because
here, you know how it is. When somebody is watching and
somebody is finding out I gave you something to eat I am in
trouble myself. When we are on that truck again I will give
you that and you can eat it.

All right so after we got pulled out and everything was clear
and we were on the truck again he said so go ahead. I ask him,
"You don't have any plates? And you don't have any spoons?"
No he says, plates I have. I have a few plates. I don't have any
spoons. I have a big spoon to put that on the plate but this is
all. But then you have to see how you get it down. So the
other seven people they were going in, their faces were everything but looking not like human bodies. Full of green beans.
Full of *Hammel* meat, and full of gravy. And I was sitting there
and I was watching that only. And he was coming to me and
said, "You know, what's going on with you?" I say, "Why?"
"Why don't you eat?" I say, "Listen, You got two eyes in your
head? Look, look what's going on there! You think this is
human? You think I would be able to get one little bit of food
down in such a situation without spoon? No." He said, "You
know you are very eh, you are very..." eh,

Gerda: Brave?

Manfred: Brave. And you behave like a bigshot. You have to.
You have to figure the situation in which you are in. But that
didn't make any matter to me. I wouldn't be able to eat for
nothing in the world. And I didn't. And then we were coming,
there was lots of food left over then and we were back at the
camp and the next day I was on that in the brickyard. I was
again at the big railroad cars working and when I was going to
work I passed him by again, that same guy from the day before. He said, "Come over! Ja, you remember me?" Ja we
were?? "Look that corner over there. I am putting in there a

bag of sandwiches, meat and good bread. When you get a chance you pick it up. I watch it that nobody is taking it because you were behaving yesterday so bravely. I think you earned it." And I had, I made a very, very nice breakfast, uh lunch that day. (*Manfred chuckles*).

Could have been the, ja, they were making things like. One day guy called me over and he was starting to, starting a conversation with me. He said, you know the whole situation, uh, we had friends in that little village where I lived and they were Jews and we were very good friends. I'm not able to understand the whole situation at all and oh he said, look there, there is a package of cigarettes outside the line behind him where he was standing. Every guy who was going over was picking up the cigarette he was a dead guy. Plain dead. Because this would be, you would be going over taking up that package of cigarettes and he would shoot you down in cold blood and the report would say...

Neil: Trying to escape?

Manfred: Ja, trying to escape a *erschossen auf der flucht* [shooting while escaping].

Neil: See this is something they had set up all the time?

Manfred: Sure. You could run into such situation always.

Neil: It was always set up?

Manfred: This was set up. Sure. There was...

Neil: Cigarettes over the line?

Manfred: No, not this was, everybody did it in a different way. You don't have to go over that line. Somebody was willing to prove you.

Neil: What kind of line was it?

Manfred: The, the, not a direct line. There was an imaginary line. It seemed like,

Gerda: A boundary?

Manfred: Ja, boundary. Every, let's say, every fifty yards was an SS man standing and the straight line from one to another guy. That was the boundary for that camp. The moment you were stepping over you were outside that concentration camp. You were willing to escape. And there were plenty of people killed there.

Another thing, one day we had, now this was getting very cold in that camp. No hat and no hair. And one day we were supposed to learn singing songs that we were able to sing when we were marching out to the camp to the clinker there and back. So one Sunday morning temperature about like here ten above, no decent clothes on your body and we had to stand under the ground for about three hours or four hours and learn songs. In the noon time when we were getting our departure from there.

We were standing maybe fifteen or eighteen thousand people out there. Fifty percent of these people got frozen hands, frozen ears, frostbites all over the body and very, very, uh, plenty of people died of head colds and such things. I myself I was a little bit, I'm a little bit a tall guy. I had a pair of underpants, long underpants and a pair of socks and the whole thing wasn't fitting right together. So I had every morning a needle and a little bit of thread and I was sewing the socks onto the long underpants 'cause I got the little bit protection for warmth. In the morning I did it and in the evening I opened it up again and the next morning I was doing the same thing. And,

Neil: You couldn't leave it that way?

Manfred: No!

Gerda: He had to get undressed.

Manfred: I had to get undressed in the evening. So different things are coming to my attention. I never will forget one day out of nowhere I was able to organize a half a loaf of bread [*Kummisbrot*]. And I was putting it in my army jacket what I had and this episode must be quite in the beginning because we didn't have any beds and we were folding our jackets and were sleeping on our jackets for a pillow. So in the evening I was going, oh and in the barrack where I was living, everybody was sleeping let's say from left to right. I was laying right at the window, at the window at the street out there. And the lamp was shining right in my face so I was laying the other way, just opposite. And this evening, with my (*to a child in background, "No, you can't have that"*), this evening, with my, with my, eh, half loaf of *Kummisbrot* [dark bread] in my pocket when I got it I was willing, I was thinking ah, let's save it for tomorrow morning. Let's have tomorrow morning a good breakfast and let's go at least once filled up and with a good feeling let's go to work a little bit with food in your body.

So in the evening and then I was going to bed and then I was laying my head on that jacket. I was thinking, my gosh, that's so hard over there, what is it? Oh, oh, that half a loaf of *Kummisbrot* now there was everything. Every good thinking for the next day was over. I was laying in that bed and I was eating that half a loaf of *Kummisbrot* and nothing in my life was tasting so good at that, uh, this was better tasting than the best piece of cake what I'm able to get now.

And just I was in the middle of that loaf of bread, a SS guy was coming and inspecting and he was seeing me laying in that bed and eating. "OUT!" So I was standing, "And that guy he's got his underpants on!" No heat. "And he's eating in bed." And he was giving it to me. I was not able to stand up anymore at the end. And you, he hit me in my face and my body and he was working at me for at least 15 hours, oh 15 minutes. "And you report tomorrow morning at your boss out there." They called it *Stubenältestete*, this was a boss.

Neil: The what?

Manfred: The oldest guy in the room. There was a boss and he was responsible. And there was nothing so worse in a concentration camp than to be recognized. When you were able to go along and you weren't picked out at the, stand out. This was the moment you were picked out and you were standing out you got the toughest time. Plenty of people in such a situation, they paid with their life. So I had to report the next day, the next morning...

Gerda: Better to be unnoticed.

Manfred: Ja, better, better to be unnoticed. So the next morning I had to report, the next morning I had to report for duty. So the guy, that all this he said to me, "You know let's find out, first time I am not willing to make any report in the main office. Let's see that guy is coming back on, when he is coming back so then I am taking it on me, you were reporting and I overlooked it to give that report in the office. When he isn't coming, forget about it." This must this thing happened maybe two or three days before my release was coming through. About this release...I am willing to talk a few words too. So we were going, he was going over it. I was going that day to work at the *Klinkerwerk* and I was coming home in the evening, nothing happened. And the next day the same thing. So they were calling me off and I was going home. So I was really lucky and I was going really around something. Um,

Neil: Now, what was the population? I mean, were there men, women and children in the camp? Or just men?

Manfred: No, only men.

Neil: Tell me that.

Manfred: The population at that camp were only men.

Neil: Only men.

Manfred: This was three or four different groups. There were in that concentration camp, the BV- criminals, then there was the witnesses of Jehovah, one group. All in separate barracks and in separate groups of barracks. Ja, Jehovah's Witnesses. Then, Dr. Niemüller, he was a very good friend of Hitler. He was a very good friend of Hitler.

Gerda: He was a friend of Hitler?

Manfred: First time he was going with the Nazis and then he turned around.

Gerda: Well then at that time he wasn't a friend of Hitler.

Manfred: No he wasn't. In the beginning he was going along with Hitler's ideas and then he was turning completely around and ja.

Neil: Communists were there?

Manfred: Communists were there and the anti-socialists, they weren't willing to work - hobos...Now I mean I was going quite fast over...

Neil: I want to go back to something.

Manfred: Ja.

Neil: I want your feelings. I want you to tell me how you felt when you arrived at the camp.

Manfred: My feelings about when I arrived in that camp, that's... it's a very, very hard thing to describe. You have to figure you are coming out of normal living conditions. You have your normal privileges. You have, you had your freedom of speech, your freedom of thinking, your freedom of behavior, completely free to behave the way you are willing to.

Then they are taking you first in that chair, then they are packing you in that truck, then they transport you to that concentration camp and there, there you see the walls and above the walls every fifty yards you see a little like a tower with a machine gun in there and above the walls you see the SS people patrolling and you are asking yourself out of nowhere, "My gosh, what have I done? I'm not a gangster. What, what is, how come that I am here in such surrounding and watched and...

Gerda: What did I do?

Manfred: What is a matter? You are not able to find an answer for this until you realize what has happened and you are finding out that you are a Jew and that is the only reason why.

Disc 2- Track One

Manfred: This is side three. Now eh...

Neil: How you felt or?

Manfred: At the end of the last tape we were just talking about my feelings when I entered that concentration camp and I was asking myself, what the heck are you doing here because you are not a criminal, you didn't do anything against the lotto, anything you have done you are born to Jewish parents, that's all, that's the whole crime you have on yourself.

Feelings? I don't know to describe my feelings. I think the most thing that was there was scared, scared stiff I should say. Because you were seeing all the Nazis you knew from outside already from what people were talking about concentration camps and what was going on in the concentration camps and doing my time as the vacuum cleaner salesman I had the chance to eh, be in one concentration camp near Leipzig where I was selling the vacuum cleaners because the commandant from there he was buying vacuum cleaners so I was a little bit informed about what was going on. I was still, this was all nothing what against what was coming up. (*He pauses for a bit*). I was scared and I, I, I really don't know...numb, numb seemed like your whole brain wasn't able to think straight and then finally after awhile I feel myself as coming up as one solution I was able to handle it. Let's wait and see what's coming up. That's the only thing you are able to do.

Um, a few other episodes in that camp. One day we were standing, no we had up on that big place the para *Platz* [place], we had countings every morning before we are going to work, from there we were ordered to our working assignments. There we could watch the people, they were called the *asozial* [anti-social]. People they were too lazy to work, let's put it really the way it is. You could see these people dying and how they were coming nearer death every day, because they were walking like drunk. Nothing to eat. They were starving for hunger. And then they had easy assignments they were in that room where they were fixing the socks, preparing the socks, and preparing the shirts, and preparing the underwear. So they had really easy assignments and in the morning at that *platz* [square], they were coming and one morning there was a guy less or two guys less, uh-huh, that's it.

They were starting and were making...No, when we were coming in that concentration camp we were coming out of normal situations. We weren't hungry and in all the surroundings in the beginning we weren't able to eat anything so we had lots of food left over. All our bread was left over and the other prisoners, they were hungry. What they were able to get for food they were taking it. So they were coming in our barracks and were begging and we were willing gladly to give it to them otherwise it was getting spoiled.

So after one or two days the Nazis were getting that, were finding it out what was going on. First time we got strictly ordered not to give any food away. Secondly, they offered every guy who got catched they would give him special treatment. They didn't say what it was but they were giving him a special treatment. Middle of November, temperature oh, twenty, twenty-five degrees like here, twenty, twenty-five degrees. So when they were catching one guy they were taking him in this bathroom, they were filling up buckets with ice-cold water and were putting that water over him from the head down. That guy was shivering. That guy was frozen half to death. And then they were sending him home. This was one treatment at the concentration camp.

Other treatments when they were later on, after we got it too and we had our own beds, and we had to make the beds and this was something for actions for the guys too. We had one thing. We had our beds for three or four days and underneath I was laying on top. The bunk beds were two layer bunk beds. I was on top and under me was a guy [who] was a very slow guy and I figured out with a piece of string to make the beds so they were one straight line. That was what the Nazis were willing to have. So I was sending him in that bathroom and I was making his bed too, only reasons for my own good not for his good, for my own good because I wasn't willing to be late and I was willing to be always ready. So that day an SS man was coming in that room and was shaking the beds. He wasn't satisfied and said, "Tonight we are having some extra tests for the beds." We were going to work in the evening, our food was coming and they had Vail meat, big, how do they call it? The big fish? The Vails?

Neil: Walleye?

Manfred: Vails?

Neil: Whales!

Mandred: Whales, the whales! They killed the whales and we got it for meat. That was tasting...the way they prepared it...it was tasting like beef. Real beef. This was a delicacy, this food what we were getting. The same evening the guy was coming when we were coming from work. The food was standing. We didn't get anything to eat. This was snowing that day. We had maybe two or three inches of snow. A barrack[with] entrance door, to your right you got your dining room, table, and the banks, banks where you were sitting on?

Neil: Planks?

Manfred: Banks?

Neil: Benches.

Manfred: Benches! Benches, ja. Benches and door to your left you got your bedroom, barrack was sixty to eighty people. So forty double bunkers one up and one down and there we were sleeping. So in the evening we were in the dining room and then he was starting an exercise with us up three windows from the dining room, three windows out in the alley between two barracks. Three windows and the whole thing was street floor only.

So he was willing to tease us and no words to describe what was happened that day. Uh, first time we were sitting at the tables we were waiting for our food then he was telling us we don't have no food and then he was starting. "On the table, on the benches, on the table, on the benches, under the tables, out of the dining room in that bedroom," and he was standing in only two small doors where everybody has to go through, forty, sixty people, sixty people in that room, forty people in that room, or eighty people in that room, forty double beds I guess. Ja, forty double beds. And he was standing with a whip at the door and was going beneath the people who were going in and then in that bedroom everybody has to go under the bed. Eighty people and only forty beds.

And then he was like opening up the windows from the dining room out in the alley, down in that snow, "Roll to your left, roll to your right, roll to your left, roll to your right." Around the barrack, running, hot, in the dining room and then under the table, underneath the table, in that bedroom, underneath the beds and he was standing always in the doors with his whip it was going beneath. I think three people died that evening in the barrack on heart attacks. Another twenty or twenty-five were seriously ill with colds and this was going on for about two or two and a half hours. This is, eh concentration camp for you.

Another thing when you were doing something wrong and you were coming back from work you have to stand at the door for two to three hours. No moving at all. Cold, no decent clothes and you have to stand there for two for three hours 'til, from six to nine. Nine was sleeping time and then you have to go to the barrack and nothing to eat and then you have to go to bed.

One day at the *klinkerwagen* a guy we were marching together. He was a very, very bad marcher so I was taking him along so he wasn't falling at the end. And there they were going with the guns against the marchers. He was working at the little … at the little railroad cart, little ones, very little ones. Where they transported that stone and that clay and some pigments and so for what they were needing for mixing the cement and so. And one of those little cars was running over him and he was on the [ground] and I was coming just to it. And everybody was crying and everybody was excited. So I was organizing a big piece of a stem, same like a tree, and we were lifting up that little truck and we were pulling him out and he was really hurt and so we were going in that *Revier*, it was same thing like a first aid station there, and there was going with him there, got him on my arm and another guy too, two guys we brought him up there and there was a *Hauptsturmführer* there, guy in charge of the whole outfit there of the concentration camp. And he was asking me, "What's a matter with him?" and I told him this happened and I think this guy is hurt and he isn't able to stand and he's badly hurt.

"Oh that's what you think, he isn't able to stand" he says, "Let him alone."

I looked at him and said "Can't you listen? Didn't you hear what I told you?"

"Let him alone and he will stand and you wouldn't believe your eyes he's standing."

And I let him alone and I wasn't believing my eyes. He was standing all right. He was standing all right. For five minutes and he was falling together and then they were bringing the ambulance and they brought him down in *Revier* [from German word *Krankenrevier*-a barrack for sick prisoners] it's a little bit in the hospital on down there and I never saw him again in that time when I was in the concentration camp. I saw him again and he was well. He was getting discharged from the concentration camp the same day I did.

So I think I would be able to go on, on such episodes for hours and hours and pages of a pages. Uh, I don't know sometimes I think this is very good not to think back...sometimes. Sometimes I think it's very good, a person has the experience, because yes you should forget, no you shouldn't forget this...I don't know.

Neil: This is our third session starting and we are up to the time when...out of the camp. Here we go.

Manfred: One more episode from the camp I have to give.

And this was in the beginning, we had, let's put it this way, I am a smoker. I like to have my cigarettes and I think this is very, very important. So for the first ten days in camp we weren't allowed to smoke.

Phone ringing in the background. Baby crying.

Manfred: After the time when we were allowed to smoke and I didn't know this was coming up the Rabbi, Rabbi Eric Cohn, he married us in Forst. He was with us in this concentration camp. He bought me the first cigarette. I think that's an experience. I was smoking that cigarette and I was nearly fainting because I lost the use to smoking and then I, keep on smoking. I say just before I would be able to go on small episodes and go on, and would never stop because when you start to think back everything is hitting your mind again and...

Neil pauses tape to do something.

Manfred: Now I wasn't talking up so far 'til our feelings. We are isolated from the world. I was a married man for three months. People were by and by getting released on different grounds. My late father in law he left the camp 20th of January and people are coming home so we start to have hope one day the whole thing would be, the whole nightmare would be over.

On the 7th of February 1939. I got my call that I was able to go home. I was very excited. I was willing to find out what was outside the walls and at about two o'clock noon, before all the formals and the bookwork (**Gerda**: "Formalities") Hmm? The formalities were finished it was about two o'clock. We were able to be released. And the last minute and the *Sturmführer* was coming to us and he was holding a speech he said, "You are getting free now. Don't think you're able to talk too much about what happened here to you in this concentration camp. You have to know one thing. The reach of the Gestapo, the reach, the hands, the arms of the Gestapo is going around the world. And when we are willing to let you out now, you have to know one thing you will be steady watched and we will always know where you are, what you are doing, how you are behaving and so on."

When we were getting our private clothes and our private things that they were taking from us when we were coming in that concentration camp nobody was able to recognize his own clothes. Because at the arriving date they were taking the whole thing and cleaning and they use stuff, clothes and everything were shrinking. So I had a pair of pants and they were reaching just above my knee. My jacket was much too short, my wallet, my leather wallet what I was getting back that was 1/5 of the original size. You couldn't use it anymore.

Gerda: Pants were above the knee??

Manfred: Below, below my knees, just below my knees. Short hair, wrinkled, whole clothes wrinkled. So the moment you were stepping outside that door and you reach freedom everybody knows where you were coming from because that was the trademarks from the concentration camps: wrinkly clothes, everything too short, no hair on your head. From there we were going to Oranienburg to the... Now another thing...before we left they wrapped lunch for us for that day.

Gerda: How many people were released?

Manfred: About thirty or forty people getting released. They were wrapping lunch for us. We were getting our money back. And when I am talking for money back there was very, very, how should I say, very touching episode that happened to me.

For Christmas we were able to send home a letter that we were able to get 30 *Marks* in that concentration camp to buy food and to have some nice Christmas parties and so I wrote my wife a letter. I didn't know what was going outside on...No, I wrote a letter to my mother in Leipzig...to my uncle in Berlin!

That's the beginning, I wrote a letter to my uncle in Berlin. He was a millionaire. He was a very rich man. He should send me 30 *Marks* in the concentration camp because my way of thinking was he was the only one able to spare that 30 *Marks*. I didn't know his whole money was frozen at the bank so he was getting only monthly allowance from the Nazis so he was in quite tight situation too. So he was writing a letter to my mother in Leipzig and told her I was writing to him about his 30 *Marks* and he would able to send 15... he's thinking. So my mother, that's the way mothers are, no thinking at all, and budget home very tight, she was taking 30 *Marks*, was running to the post office was paying in 30 *Marks* for me on telegraph, same like here, by wire, ja, by wire, that's it. The rule in concentration camp was nobody was getting money that was sent by wire. So I had 30 *Marks* in the front office and in the concentration camp I didn't have any money.

So on my day of release I got that 30 *Marks* with me. Then we went to Oranienburg. There we took the train, elevated train to the Jewish Community Center in Berlin in Oranienbug, Schlösser. And, there we got greeted. We got registered who was coming out and this was just the biggest contrast, one of the biggest contrast what was happening to me. There we were coming out of the concentration camp pressure, always danger, always on your watch so things don't happen to you. There it was a really nice, lovely and friendly atmosphere. Young married women were giving their service, nicely dressed and tables decorated with every trimmings, white tablecloths. They had a cup of coffee and they were able to eat. I couldn't get one bite down and there I wasn't eating anything. I had a cup of coffee and that was it. And everybody was coming to me and now, "What is going on? Why didn't you eat?" No, I can't eat. I have to calm down and adjust again.

And there I made one resolution. I wasn't willing for the future, on the 7th of February, to eat anything. I was fasting. I fasted for quite awhile of years. And later on so in this I wasn't able to anymore, doctor's order I should stop that. From there I called my wife. I sent a cable to my wife that I was released and that I was arriving in Frankfurt/Aurora late in the evening. I also called my boss...

Gerda talking in background.

Manfred: In Forst, I would be in our town. Then I called my boss, Dr. Lehmann, the company, the credit house that I was working for and I reached him and I told him where I am and he was very happy and he was asking me was he able to do anything for me and so I told him my clothes are terrible. I don't have any coat. I don't have any hat. I don't have...my suit isn't fitting anymore and so two and a half hours later he reached Oranienburg-Schlösser and he bought me completely different outfit and clothes and so I wasn't pinpointed, marked on where I was coming from. So in the evening I left by train, train ride from about, in the afternoon I left the train ride from about two and a half or three hours. I reached Frankfurt/Aurora and I left the train and there was my wife picking me up from the train.

Gerda: And you had to change trains.

Manfred: I had to change trains. I had to transfer in Frankfurt/Aurora and I had to take the train and there was my wife. Everything up 'til then I was mentioning it was to my liking, she brought it along in a big bag, in a market bag, little suitcase. Cigarettes-Attica, bananas, grapes, chocolate and walnuts, peanuts. If I was saying I am liking peanuts, everything what I just mentioned in my life before it was in that bag and she was going around me like she had to get adjusted too that I was back again three months married. So then we went home and I remember when I was coming home friends of ours (the husband was in the concentration camp too) they were home and on my way from the train station to my house was about ten minutes walk. So my wife she was willing to do anything for me, so the first thing I said to her, "Listen, give me that key.

Give me the keys to the house and give me the key to the house door, to the apartment door and to the house door."

I like to take over again, let's put it this way. Then I reached that house and there a friend, friends of ours, and one was in the kitchen and she was making *Wienerschnitzel* for me bigger than a dinner plate. I said, "Who would be able to eat this?" She said "You eat, you don't have good things to eat for a long time." No, no I wouldn't be able. I wasn't eating that early anything. This morning my lunch they wrapped from the concentration camp I was giving away because I couldn't eat. Emotional upset, I couldn't eat at all. And then from that *Wienerschnitzel* I was cutting off maybe a quarter of that schnitzel.

I was eating a little bit in the evening and then I was going in the bedroom and I saw the big wardrobe what we have standing there the ways in Germany partly for clothes, partly for handkerchiefs, and underwear, and shirts and such things. And I was standing on that wardrobe, I was opening the door and thought, "Oh look, such a richedom!" There you have handkerchiefs and there you have underwear to change and there you have undershirts and over shirts and heavy shirts and light shirts, pajamas, and shoes and house shoes. This was not to describe this feeling and the emotion I had was it. Then we settle. In the evening we get visits from a couple friends from concentration camp and then we were talking and how the situation was out there and what was going on in between time when we were in that concentration camp.

Neil: Okay, what were the conditions under which you were released? How did you get out in the first place?

Manfred: I have to find that out. No, no, I am coming to that. Now there were... (*talking in the background*) Sure. Why not? Then there was...Then we were talking, then I was resting a little bit, and then I was going to bed. Because the next day morning, early, I had to report every day, once a week to the

Gestapo. I was out for, I got released from the concentration camp for three months and this was a time in three months I had to emigrate from Germany. I had to get out of Germany.

Now two or three days later we went to visit my parents in Leipzig and there I was getting the reason and the circumstances why I was getting out of that concentration camp. Sure - from Leipzig. You knew it? (*Neil talking in background*) Let's put it this way. In Leipzig we were talking about it and it was coming out. A brother-in-law of mine his brother was married to my sister (they were killed in Warsaw in the Ghetto, Ghetto fight), he got a very good friend and she was secretary to the Argentine Consul in Leipzig. She was talking German, the consul wasn't talking German at all, so she was taking letters from the Gestapo in Frankfurt/Aurora and the order from where they were coming. She was sending letters in German to the consulate in Frankfurt/Aurora.

Neil speaking in background.

Manfred: 'Cause the Gestapo in Frankfurt/Aurora are declaring *Heftlink*, number, prisoner's number so and so, his name and number, he is supposed to be on special date in Leipzig and the Argentine consul expects.

Neil in the background.

Manfred: This is side four. Now I learned the way I was released from the concentration camp. I had to order through a girlfriend of my brother-in-law. She was the secretary of the Argentine consul and she was putting in the mail, on the consul's desk, letters in German, addressed to the Gestapo in Frankfurt/Aurora regarding prisoner number so and so, that he is supposed to be at the Argentine Consulate in Leipzig on a special date, expects working and immigration to Argentine. And that's the way I was coming out and that is the same way I was later going from Forst to Leipzig to give help to other prisoners that still were in.

So I visited my parents and when we reached home and my parents weren't coming to the railroad station picking me up because I lived over twenty years in Leipzig, I knew everything. You went home. I'm coming. This isn't a strain. They were standing at the streetcar stop and were waiting and when I was coming out from that streetcar my mother was embracing me and wasn't willing to let me go at all. This was nearly a disaster, "Come on mom. Be a good girl" and I was calming her down and then we were going up and I was staying for two days in Leipzig and then we were going home again.

From then on I was starting, from then on, I had three months time, I was starting on my emigration out of Germany. I hadn't anything going for me and when you start to work with the consulate for emigration this needs time and time, and changing letters. And when you live in a small town where there isn't any consulate, so I was going daily from Forst to Berlin and for European and German thinking [it's] a long way of traveling.

Neil: How many miles?

Manfred: For American thinking that's the way from Milwaukee to Chicago.

Neil: One hundred miles.

Manfred: One hundred miles. Here everybody has his car and everybody is sitting in that car and two, two and half hours later everybody's in Chicago.

Neil: One way? One way? Two hundred miles a day.

Manfred: So I was going daily (**Neil**: One way?) Ja. So I was going daily to Berlin was starting to work on my emigration. There was only one way out of Germany and this was Shanghai, China. Because you don't need, you didn't need anything immigration papers, [the] only thing you need was ship ticket from Trieste to Shanghai and there you're on your own.

Gerda: Traveled by boat.

Manfred: Ja, boat ticket. That's what I said. So I was starting to work I was working with German lines, with Italian lines, with the *Lloyd Triestino*. Then after I was going for about three weeks I was starting to have a little bit results. First time the situation was there I didn't have any money to buy for the ticket. So the Jewish Organizations the *Hilfsverein*, it's translated, the Jewish Aid for Immigration, let's put it this way, ja. So they were promising me to pay the ship tickets. (*Gerda in background speaking.*) Third, when no other chances of second class to Shanghai. So I worked and I never will forget it. We were going from different people from Leipzig we are going, from, from Forst. I never will forget ending April there was a guy I was working always on *Lloyd Triestino* he was coming and he told me he, there is a possibility and I could have tickets in case one family with three people them like we are, not able to go, then we could jump in. We should make everything ready. We should have customs things ready. We should have eh…we should be packed and should be ready to go. And I was starting. I was starting to make customs and everything ready. Now in between life was going…

Gerda: This was first class tickets.

Manfred: Ja, this is a first class ticket. So from there I was, I was going back to the Jewish Organizations and there we had a big fight and there was a guy, his name was…

Gerda: No! No names!

Manfred: Okay, no names. There was a guy and he was thinking all the money was going for help and the Jewish people he's paying this out his own pocket and he was very rude and very high on top and he was willing to, to, he was willing to let us feel we are beggars, let's put it this way. And my caseworker, he was a very nice guy. He said to me, "You don't lose your temper. And I promise you we have a meeting at one o'-clock noon you could be here again, you could be here again at three-thirty in the afternoon and you get a resolve." At three-thirty I was at the HELP (Hilfsverein) organization again.

Neil: Speak in the microphone. (*pause*) Speak in the microphone.

Manfred: Ja. And I was three-thirty again at the organization and there he was coming and he was telling me okay they're putting up that money for first class tickets for me and I should wait and I can go right away to the *Lloyd Triestino* and can make everything ready. So I was waiting and one signature and one part of the whole thing has to be, has to be done, from Mr., from that other guy, that rude guy. And I was waiting, and waiting, and waiting and waiting and time was getting short. I had fifteen or twenty minutes bus ride from there to where *Lloyd Triestino* was and...

Phone ringing in the background. Baby crying.

Manfred says to Neil - No, stop it there. *TAPE STOPS.*

Manfred: So there wasn't any result and then I was losing my patience. And I was willing to rush in his office and I was willing to give him a piece of my mind. And that waiting room was full of people and everybody was watching me and was, what was going on. Then I got him out and then I told him what he should give me his way of thinking. This isn't on my free will that I am here, that I am begging for that ticket. I was three months in the concentration camp and he was sitting here outside he didn't know what was going on in the world. He is behind these four walls and reading only everything from the newspaper. I was in the middle in, I am willing to get out of here and every chance I am able to get I will take and I think this is his duty that he is giving me that helping hand because this is his job and this is what he get paid for. And was just so far that the big real fist fight was going to start and my case worker was coming out and he was calming me down and he was taking me in his office and he said, "Mr. Oelsner, let me tell you something. You don't have to do anything anymore in this case. You don't have to go to nobody anymore. I'm taking over completely for you and I'm finishing up everything for you and I am promising you and I give you the guarantee you will have everything in time. Ten minutes later I had all my papers and ten minutes later I left *Hilfsverein* on bus on my way to *Lloyd Triestino*, ship line.

Neil: What is it, Lloy?

Manfred: *Lloyd Triestino*

Gerda saying something in background.

Manfred: Shipline.

Neil: An Italian ship line.

Manfred: Ja, *Lloyd Triestino*. I arrived there and I was proud, I was very proud to have accomplished something and I was putting down my papers to my caseworker there to the guy, to the agent who was selling the tickets. And he said, "Just a minute, Mr. Oelsner. I am going through the papers and I will let you know right away about this". Ten minutes later he was coming back and he said, "This is amazing what you have accomplished there. You are the first guy getting out from *Hilfsverein* boat tickets first class, but this is no good at all. Because the whole thing is written for you." Didn't mean anything. *Hilfsverein* have to give us the same papers written in our name that we are able to get that money from the bank. The whole thing is *Spercherdau* , just (**Neil**: Tied up.) tied up money from the Nazis. The whole money from the *Hilfsverein* was from the Jewish H stations were locked and were only able to get money out for relief or payments of boat tickets and so. So I couldn't do anything anymore the same day. I was going home and I was real happy about the whole situation. Now I think I'm coming back what was going on because in between time there is time, time to cover from about two months what was going on in our little town and how we were living and what we were doing and how we were in our way fighting against the Nazis and fighting for our, for our existence.

Tape Stops.

Manfred: So now we are starting our first session, (*Gerda talking in background*), with that, with my life story. Coming back to the end what I said in the last session, about the time from two months to cover what was going on in our little town, by that I mean, what we were supposed to do under pressure from the Nazis and how we were coming over the time because with the things I had accomplished in Berlin, time was coming closer and closer that we were able to leave Germany. Now a little town, after I was coming home from concentration camp I had to go once a week to the police station for check up cause I was still in Forst, cause I was not willing to flee the country. When I was coming back my work with the company was still going on. My boss, Dr. Lehmann, he was still liquidating, and was willing to get the, eh, so much money as possible from his business back. I don't know if I told this story already or not.

Seventh of February I was coming out of the concentration camp. Twenty-first of February was my wife's birthday. This was the first birthday in our marriage. So I promised her I will stay home because from time to time I was going to Leipzig. My parents lived there and that Argentine consulate was in Leipzig and this way we were bringing out from concentration camp *Sachsenhausen* between twelve and fifteen younger Jewish people. Probably part, a few of them were going to Palestine and were going all over the world. So I promised my wife that I will stay home, that I was willing to celebrate that birthday with her, because that was the first one in our marriage life. First evening before, next morning, neighbors of mine there was still two boys in *Sachsenhausen* and his father was coming to me and was begging me I should go and should try to do something 'cause the boys not coming out, because time start to run out and situation is getting tighter and tighter because for that Second World War was coming up. This was already in the sky... already in the air so. He was coming up tomorrow at about eight-thirty in the morning. We lived about ten minutes walking distance from the train station and eight-thirty was that and nine-fifteen was the train leaving to Leipzig so after he was begging me and he was talking over the situation with me so I decided I will be back in the evening and I was going to Leipzig and I was making the papers for the boys ready. And two weeks later they were home.

Life, uh, was going on. We were living quite scared and because I was out on limited time, I should be ready to leave the country 1st of May, 1939. Otherwise they promised me they will take me back in that concentration camp. So this time I was, all of us, we were living quite under pressure and we had to accomplish something and from the beginning and we don't know how there was no enough money to do something. We didn't have any work started for emigration papers. There's lots of work involved. Then, I said it before, Shanghai was only, the only place on Earth where someone was able to immigrate to. All you need was that boat ticket.

So, in that little town with all the families after that concentration camp incident the whole little Jewish community was closer together and everybody was willing to give the next one a helping hand. And so we were living scared, but we were living and we still had a little bit social gathering. We were playing our skat [card game] parties, our skat evenings, with the rabbi and with friends same before. And we were going once in while over the weekend home to my parents. And so we were reaching the time at about end of April, this is the time now I am coming back to Berlin, to the *Lloyd Triestino* and to my boat ticket for Shanghai. The guy promised me there the whole thing should go, the whole papers from the Jewish, not from the Jewish, from the HELP from the aid station should go on the name of the *Lloyd Triestino* and he promised me when I am bringing the paper in her name I would get the tickets to Shanghai. So 1st of May it's a holiday in Germany, this is same like Labor Day. They are celebrating their 1st of May. This is the day of the working people, let's put it this way. They put up the Maibaum [Maypole in America] and they are dancing around and they are drinking and they are enjoying theirself.

Then on the 2nd of May, I left with ... to fix my papers and then I got everything fixed and I was coming to the *Lloyd Triestino* and I was asking for my case worker there who was knowing everything and they told me this guy had a motorbike accident over the weekend and they didn't know anything about it. So there was quite another fight going on about it. It is here, was here already, he sent money for the boat tickets and I was working for the *Conte Verde*, that was the name of the boat, and I had already my cabin numbers and everything, and then finally I was coming so far that the whole thing was fixed up. In the evening of May 2nd I left, I was going back to Forst with the tickets. I don't know I was talking about, they told me from *Lloyd Triestino* I should fix up everything and I should have everything packed so that we are able to leave in the last minute with notice of two or three days and so I did it.

In the same building where I lived, in the same apartment building where I lived, was guy living, a custom inspector who was inspecting everything that was put in, what was packed and he was with there and nothing was going out which wasn't with permission from the Nazi government. He knows me and he was, I mean we lived together in that house one, one and half years, and he was very friendly guy. I should say he was everything as up on Nazi. The condition were going over his head and so he was going along because he was a government position. So he was up there and when we wrapped everything and then he was going out, three, four, five hours. Over noon we were packing the whole thing for two days, he was four-five hours out and we were able to, we didn't have anything, when in case we had anything we were willing to get everything, anything, something out of the country it would be very easy. So we had everything ready when I was coming home for, with the tickets, 2nd of May. Then next morning I was going to the custom once more because they were picking up the boxes. This was to my, to my....hmmm?

Gerda: Movers.

Manfred: To the movers and they fixed up everything. My landlord I was giving notice there is a possibility that I was able to go out with the government agencies with checks what you all need with the papers. This was everything fixed as I was able to get everything on short notice.

Neil: What did the police say?

Manfred: Police, uh, police was the Gestapo. This was the Nazi, the main position from the Nazis in that little town, police.

Neil: But they...

Manfred: They knew it. They knew everything and I was doing everything with permission because I had to get permission to get everybody out of the city that I was able to go to Berlin for working for the boat tickets. Then is coming a very, very dark episode. I think we left Forst, 1st of May,

Gerda talking in background.

Manfred: We left Forst, 3rd or 4th of May we left Forst. Then we were staying five days with my parents.

Gerda: The boat left. When did the boat leave?

Manfred: Oh I am a little bit mistaken. The boat left June 6th, June...

Gerda: Shut this off.

Manfred: Shut it off. *TAPE STOPS.*

Manfred: Now the whole thing is cleared up. We left Forst 3rd of May and we were going to Leipzig to my parents and we were staying four days I guess with my parents and we left Leipzig 7th of May by train. We were going first to Munich and we were staying overnight and then we were going to Trieste and there we arrived on the 9th of May, late evening we arrived. We were going right away on the boat and on the morning of the 10th of May we left Trieste. This is the departure.

Now we were staying four days with my parents in Leipzig. Everybody my parents knew we were going out of the country. We were knowing we were going out. There was no words spoken about what was supposed to be happened when we are, when we left 7th of May. Everybody knew that this was a goodbye with no reunion again and everybody knows this is the last thing we were seeing of each other. (*long pause*) Everybody was nervous. Everybody was excited. Everybody was scared. My parents, especially my mother, she was one hundred percent knowing what was happening. She wasn't able to talk much about everything. We were behaving like we were there for a short visit and no, no nothing, nothing was spoken.

After we left, after we left Leipzig and we arrived late evening at the 9th of May in Trieste, we were going on the boat and were going to sleep and in the morning when we were awake we were already on our way.

Gerda talking in the background.

Manfred: My wife was very scared about that whole trip and so she said, "Oh, let's go to bed." And in the morning when we are getting awake we are now away and so it was the way.

DISC 2 -Side 2

Manfred: After all that crucial situations, I, was and we were living through the last two or three months in Germany and we reached that boat. We were able to breathe more freely again. We knew Italy was a partner with Germany; still we were reaching slow and safe freedom, at least freedom of movement, freedom of speech.

Twenty-six, how many? Twenty-six? Twenty-six on the *Conte Verde*. I should say this was the time of my life. First class looks this boat. First class, eh, eh food. First class accommodation. Air conditioned room. This was 1939 already. Timeless bottles with ice cold water, when someone was going in our compartment, there was someone taking a bath, washing his hands, using some towels and we were going out and ten minutes later we were coming back the whole thing was fixed. The tub was filled with water again. First class service. Beautiful cabin.

Gerda: We had above sea cabins.

Manfred: Above the main deck we had our cabins above the main deck and so we were. Beautiful trip. No trouble with too much rough sea. Beautiful trip. Food-mornings first class breakfast for our way of living. Our way of living terrific because we had meat, tongue and scrambled eggs in the morning and lots of meats and fried chicken. What you were able to think of you could eat because there was a menu cart in for breakfast fifty, sixty, seventy different things to eat for *Tiffin* [*lunch*].

Gerda: Five meals a day.

Manfred: Five meals a day. You could have sixty to seventy things for dinner. It was out of the world. Now the whole thing was, uh, without going in the dining room was without any condition. You were able to go in the dining room the way you are. So I had bought money, 900 German *Marks*. At this time was a lot of money.

Neil: Is that from the Hilfs group?

Manfred: Ja, ja I signed for that. Ja. Uh, uh, so we were coming in tropical climate. It was very hot and we bought completely different outfits, shorts. We never wore shorts before from this time and for the next ten years, shorts shouldn't leave me because this was the outfit in Shanghai. We were running around in shorts and short sleeve shirts. This was it. We were dressed and the boat was the same thing. We bought mostly everything in white. White shirts, white shorts and we were looking quite nicely dressed. After about four or five days,

Gerda: Probably younger to wear that stuff...they didn't know where to go.

Neil: Yeah sure.

Manfred: Ah ja, I'm just coming it.

Neil: Now where, wait, yeah, young enough to enjoy it. Yeah? Now where was the ticket to from Trieste to where?

Manfred: Shanghai.

Neil: Well, you could have got off anywhere along the way.

Manfred: No, no, no, no, no, no, no,

Neil: You could have stayed in ah...

Manfred: The reason I am coming to it. The reason I couldn't stay there because the English consulate [sic] wasn't open. They had to give me permission for immigrating to there.

Neil: Then you had to go on.

Manfred: Sure. So,

Neil: We're almost to it this time. Go ahead.

Manfred: So...uh, after three of four days there was coming and I think that was in Aden shortly before we were going in the Suez Canal was coming the consul from Italy on the boat and they were starting to have formal conditions in the dining room, for dinner, at least for dinner. So uh, I told my steward, "Do you have to, do you have to make different arrangements, because I am not on that boat for a pleasure trip? I'm lucky enough to have first class tickets and I'm enjoying everything and everything is good." What?

Neil and Gerda talking in the background.

Disc 3- Side One

Manfred: This is side 5.

Neil: You telling a story or other arrangements.

Manfred: Now...Junior take the mittens off.

(Lots of laughter)

Manfred (*still laughing*): So we were just talking about the consulate from Italy was coming on the boat. He was going to Colombo and they were starting to make formal arrangements for dinner, dress up and I was talking with my steward and I told him, uh, I'm not willing to have every, any pleasure on me because I'm enjoying that boat trip and first class. I'm lucky enough. This is not a pleasure trip, because I don't know what is waiting for me in Shanghai, what is coming up, so I am not willing to celebrate. I'm willing to have everything quiet and without celebrations. So he was sending me the head waiter and I was told him the same story and he, uh I told him...

Gerda: You told him you don't want to be formal dressed to go to the dining room. (*Neil speaking in background.*)

Manfred: (*responding to Gerda and Neil*) Sure, I told this already. I'm not willing to have any pressure. I'm not willing to get dressed formal in the dining room and he told me I don't know what we are doing. That's alright with me I'm, I mean I think I paid for using the dining room when you have the pressure with formal dining, serve me in my cabin. All right he says I will. Half hour, three quarters of an hour he was calling for me again over the loud speaker and he was talking to me I was thinking it over, this is much too much commotion for us, we are serving you in your cabin. We have to find another solution. Okay, another solution?

Gerda: They need about four waiters.

Manfred: They need four waiters to serve us in our, for three persons, my father-in-law, my wife and me.

"So uh, what do you found for resolution?"

"In case this is okay for you. We have two calls for breakfast, we have two calls *tiffin*, and we have two calls for dinner. The first call for breakfast is six-thirty. The second call for breakfast is seven-thirty. When would you be coming in the dining room at eight o'clock? Would this be alright with you for breakfast?"

"That's alright with me for breakfast. Okay."

Gerda in background talking.

Manfred: (*Responding to Gerda*) Oh ja well. Oh, okay. Ja. Still for dinner, *tiffin* and for dinner, for *tiffin* too. No? Only for dinner? Okay, only for dinner. So he says the first two calls for dinner, first call at six-thirty, and the second call at seven-thirty and you would come at eight o'clock in the dining room, this would be all right with us, okay. And so we did. We had nearly the whole dining room to ourselves. So we were coming for dining and I was able to enjoy my food. I didn't have any pressure and I don't have to, I don't have that feeling by myself I'm celebrating something where I didn't know which way I am going.

When we were going on boat we had a few formalities we checked our boat money what we had, so we had 900 *Marks* boat money and we had the registrate and we had to give our position and they were bringing our luggage in boat partly in our cabins and partly in the luggage room. Big luggage room down, far down in the boat. So, uh, we fixed everything and then we start to enjoy our trip. We were sitting up in the highest decks. There was a swimming pool. There was a little bit bar. We were able to get cold drinks.

And the whole boat was ninety percent immigrants that were going to Shanghai, so. We were sitting in groups during the day, we were sitting in the evening we were singing songs. We were having little bit music up in that highest deck there in that little, little like a bar, little dance room and the swimming pool. And we had a marvelous time on board. Marvelous. After two and a half or three weeks it's that big dinners that we had we didn't know what to eat anymore. We were eating reganal (**Gerda**: Regional), regional specialities. Always in which part of the world we were. We were going, our trip was from Trieste, Aden, Suez Canal, to Bombay, Calcutta, Singapore, (**Neil**: Colombo) Colombo,

Gerda: Colombo, Singapore.

Manfred: Colombo, Singapore, Ceylon.

Neil: Hmm?

Manfred: We were of Ceylon.

Neil: Ce va? That's Colombo.

Manfred: Oh Colombo, ja. Hong Kong.

Gerda: Hong Kong, Singapore.

Manfred: Singapore, Hong Kong, Hong Kong, Shanghai. So eh,

Neil: The order is off there. You stopped at every one of those?

Manfred: We stopped. We didn't have permission to go on land in (**Gerda**: Aden) Singapore, in Aden, in Port Said.

Gerda: What did you say? Just a moment (*to Neil*) We did not have permission? (**Manfred**: No. We didn't.) We did not have permission to go on land in Port Said, Aden and Bombay. (*Manfred*: In Bombay) We could go in Colombo and Singapore.

Manfred: In Colombo and Singapore we were on land. The first stops we didn't get any permission to leave the boat so the Jewish Organizations from that towns they were coming on boat and they were finding out what we were in need for and they were willing to help and you had food and everything on boat there were still other problems and then they were coming on boat and were finding out what was going on. First step on land was Singapore. In Singapore,

Gerda: No Colombo first.

Manfred: Oh Colombo first, yeah. Now with all my, now coming back with all my boat money what I had, I didn't have any chance to spend all that money and I was willing to leave it there so they had something like a little bit souvenir store and store with goods what you were able to use on the boat so I bought three cameras and I bought a few bottles of liquor and I bought English cigarettes in tin cans fifty piece: Gold Flake, Lucky Strike, Navy Cut Capstan, and Navy Cut Player's, and uh.

Well first I started in Colombo we were going on land, I was taking along the three cameras first. And uh, we were going down in the morning and I was willing to find out we were able to sell the cameras I was able to make some money. We sold the cameras. I got three pounds, one pound per camera. An English pound this time was about five American dollars so this was fifteen American dollars. I never was so rich in my life before because we were going out from Germany and we were only able, we only get permission to take out four American dollars per person. So all our belonging and money up to Colombo was what we had on board money and twelve American dollars.

Neil: And a little bit of Italian lirae, you said before.

Manfred: And yeah, I forgot one thing, and this is a very cute and interesting thing. I had a few Italian liras because in Trieste, they were from the Jewish organizations and harbor and they were giving us a little bit spending money. And I saved this in Aden, in Port Said, in Port Said the people were surrounding our big boat, the *Conte Verde,* with small boats and they had different kinds of goods, of leather goods and of food, and of vegetables and they were willing to make business with the people on board. So I was starting to deal with one guy for leather bags and I bought with my Italian money with what I had in Port Said, three handbags. They make it here now in the States too. This is like...

Gerda: Tooled leather.

Manfred: Tooled leather. Tooled.

Gerda: (*overpronouncing*) Tooled.

Manfred: Tooled leather, this is some motif and it same like burned in. So I bought three such bags and I put it in my cabin and I forgot everything about it. So when we were in Colombo, first time we were going down and I sold the three cameras for three dollars.

Neil: Three dollars?

Manfred: For three pounds. Then I had 200 German *Marks*. I took this down and I sold this for five English pounds. This is about twenty American dollars, this was about 84 German *Marks* I was getting out of 200. Then I brought down cigarettes. I was selling English cigarettes in Colombo for about an English pound. And my handbags, my three handbags I sold this in Colombo for forty Shanghai dollars. This, by this time, six Shanghai dollars was in American dollars, this was about seven American dollars too. So I made a little bit money in Colombo, what my story will tell I was able to use in Shanghai, very, very good.

Neil: Maybe we should stop now.

Manfred: Ja.

Neil: Stop?

Manfred: Stop. This is end of session four.

Manfred: This is session number five, 4th of July, 1967. After we, I had my business, what for later time will prove was very successful, finished in Colombo, we were going on boat again. And eh, we were going on our trip. Our next stop, life on boat was going on as usual. We had beautiful weather. We had wonderful accommodations. We had beautiful, beautiful time, very, very wonderful time on the boat. The next stop was Bombay?

Gerda: No, Singapore!

Manfred: Singapore was the next stop. There we went on, we were able to go on land and uh, my wife, she had to do some shopping she was willing to buy some thread because she had something to fix. We were in the store there and the boss himself he was waiting on us and he was finding out that we were foreigners and we were talking with our little bit of English what we know. Then we find out he was a Jewish fellow too. He invited us for dinner. He was married to a Malayan wife and he was going with us. First time he was showing us all of Singapore. He was showing us the temple in Singapore. He was showing us the town and the city, and the part where the jungle was starting with all the monkeys there. And then we were going in his house for dinner. We had a wonderful Malayan dinner. In our conversation he was starting to like me very much and he was willing to keep me in Singapore. He was trying to get connection with the British consulate in Singapore. The day was a holiday. In Europe they call it, eh...

Gerda: Mid-Summer holiday.

Manfred: Pentecost is what they call it here. And that English consulate was closed. So he promised me he will work on it. I should go on to Shanghai. When he got all of the papers and everything for immigration to Singapore ready then he will call me back. I think it was, for the moment, it was looking very, very bad thing. This was holiday in the Pentecost holiday, for future this was coming out, this was very, very lucky for me. Then Singapore was, then during the war taking from the Japanese and all the...

Gerda: By the Japanese.

Manfred: By the Japanese and all the people were making that very terrible German march,

Neil: Not from Singapore. No?

Manfred: Ja, they still made it from Singapore too. They transported the people from Singapore for the Germans.

Neil: Oh they did? There too?

Manfred: Ja, there too. (**Neil**: Oh!) So this was a very, very lucky thing for me that the consulate was closed. So we were spending a very nice day in Singapore from the morning to the evening and in the evening we left Singapore again and we were going to Shanghai. I can't remember that we had on our whole trip very bad weather. We had a little bit high seas but nothing very, very...(**Gerda**: No stormy weather.), no stormy weather. Then our next stop was Hong Kong. In Hong Kong there was waiting at the boat a German guy. And uh...

Gerda: Not Jewish.

Manfred: Not Jewish. He was not Jewish. He was a German guy and he was taking from all the boats that were coming from Germany that they were stopping in Hong Kong, he was inviting people over, people in a restaurant. He was serving at his own cost, German food and beer and he was willing to have a little bit company. He must be, he must be lived for a long period of time in Hong Kong and he was very lonesome and he was homesick so he was willing to find out where the people were coming from and what condition they were living in Germany and what towns and few people were there were coming very close neighborhoods. Free beer, free food and he was paying the transportation to and from the boat. So we spent a very nice evening there and then next day we were going on our last stretch to Shanghai.

Now after we were living four weeks on that boat in very luxurious conditions and we were arriving in Shanghai. I never in my life saw such a big contrast that the conditions of the boat and Shanghai itself. This is the first impression. We were going through custom and when we were ready, we don't have much. When we were ready we don't have any accommodations or Jewish Welfare Fund in Shanghai they were giving us board and shelter in the refugee camps. And our camp was Chaoufoong Heim. This was same like in a big church before, so same like missionary school.

Gerda: Missionary. C-H-A-O-

Neil: How's it spelled? Spell it now.

Manfred: C-H-A-O-U-F-O-O-N-G.

Manfred: So they were, they had a big truck, an open truck, side boards on it and then they were boarding on that truck about between forty and fifty people and up they were going to the Chaoufoong *Heim*. That feeling you were traveling on that boat in comfort and you were riding on that bus is no comfort at all. One was clinging to the other one so nobody was falling from that truck. And we were completely down because this was already a sign of what was coming up. So we were, it was about from the bund where we arrived, (**Gerda**: Bund.) from the Bund to the Chaoufoong-*Heim* was about 20 to 25 minutes truck ride.

Neil: From the Bund. What's the Bund?

Manfred: Bund - this is the main street where the harbor side of Shanghai. All the big banks and all the big corporations they have the offices. A very, very beautiful street that bund in Shanghai. And um, in Chaoufoong *Heim* we were called in the office, we were making our registration and then guide was coming and showing us our room. Barracks, same like barracks, big rooms. Oh, forty-fifty double beds, bunk beds, no space in between, one bed at another one.

There we are living oh, about forty or fifty married couples in that room. You have a very small space to put one or two of your trunks, and to have your daily things what you are willing to use, your clothes for daily use and you don't have to cook because they were giving three meals, breakfast, lunch and dinner. So this was very, very primitive. I am not willing go into the smaller life affairs. They were coming up. We didn't stay long in there because we were feeling very uncomfortable and I have a little bit, I was, I'm coming to it. I was working so we moved in a smaller room where we were three couples and two bachelors, so it was much more comfortable. (*Gerda and Manfred laugh*).

Gerda talks in background.

Manfred: So the first two or three days in that Chaoufoong camp we, I feel myself I was looking around. I was trying to get acquainted. I was trying to get a little bit an idea what was going and how we should live and what we should do and what's the best way to come, to stay over water, let's put it this way. We were talking with the people there and we were starting to make friends and we were getting acquainted.

So with the next boat what was coming I was finding out there were two or three guys bringing in all the luggage from the newcomers to their spaces where they were stored. And they were collecting for smaller luggage ten cents, for bigger twenty cents, for bigger forty and fifty cents. So after two or three days I was starting to go along there and start to work. With the second boat that was coming I was already working. And one day, the first day I was handling the luggage I think I made six or seven dollars which was plenty of money for Shanghai. This was only I think twice a month. This was money only twice a month. So I was putting in the registration for that work commando to keep that travel *Heim* in place, in order.

Gerda: Clean.

Manfred: Clean. So I was start to work always commando in that....

Gerda and Neil talking in background.

Neil: Clean up? Maintenance.

Manfred: Ja, maintenance. I was starting to work in the maintenance in the Chaoufoong-*Heim*. We get paid thirty dollars a month and everything free. You had to work sometimes 10, 12, 14, 15 hours a day. You had to watch, you had duty at the door sometimes in the evening because it was isolated. Only people that were living in there were able to come in. When the second boat was coming in I bought a little bit a two-wheeler hand truck. And then we start to make, we start to take the bigger pieces that are forty and fifty cents a piece and I was starting to...

Gerda: Hand cart.

Manfred: Hand cart, ja, a hand cart, a two-wheeler. Two hands on it, little bit iron, wood and iron pieces on it. A little cart. Then I start to make, when the people move out, they moved in private homes, then we were bringing them with our cart, Chusan Road, Chaoufoong Road, Dal'ny Road and all the streets there. Usually we would charge three dollars for one transport, for a little cart filled we would charge three dollars. So this was going on for about...we arrived in Shanghai 6th of June, 1939. This was going on still ending the year, 'til November. For the first 9th of November party, the 9th of November commemoration. There was a big rally at a Kinchow Road...(**Gerda**: In another camp), in another camp, Kinchow Road. We went there and then a relative of mine, distant relative was living in that home and so we visited him and we were listening to the speech that was going on and then we walked home. On the way home I passed by...

Gerda: He came along.

Manfred: He came along and he told me, "Look there! They're building something like a refugee business. Maybe this is something for you." And I was going in and I was talking and there was a tobacco store for rent. No idea...

Gerda talking in background.

Manfred: No idea how to buy cigarettes. No idea how much profit was on it. Okay I was there. I was making my down payment. I got twenty dollars on me that day. I was renting that store for eighty dollars month for rent. Then I was digging in and was finding out how the whole business is done. You have to find your places where you'll buy. You have to know all the kinds and the trademarks of cigarettes. And you have....and then I opened that up. The whole thing was ten stores, a pharmacy, a beauty store, a leather store, and grocery store, and a store for your toys, cigars and cigarettes..

Neil: Was it like a little shopping center?

Manfred: Ja it was a little...

Gerda: (*chuckles*) In a room like this they had eight different stores.

Manfred: The room was double like this. The store was around the corner and there was the egg handle and there was the barber...ja stores. So...every other month one of the stores was falling asleep. Couldn't make a living.

Gerda: Going out of business.

Manfred: They were...a soldier isn't dying, he is just, yes...fading away. So every other month one of these businesses was fading away. Then the landlord couldn't hold that house so he was selling that house. Russian he bought that house and made three stores out of it. I was willing to stick to it because I don't have another chance. So he was coming to me first and he was saying,

"When you, how would it be you are taking the corner?"

"Yeah, I'm taking the corner. All right. How much is it rent?"

"Oh hundred dollars a month."

"All right."

Gerda speaking in the background.

Manfred: Forty, no eighty, one hundred dollars a month, I'll take it. Then the middle store that was first, the middle part he was renting right away to a Chinese botcher.

Neil: A what? Butcher?

Manfred: Butcher. Ja, Chinese butcher. And the third store he put the window on. All our stores were open. Bolt by bolt, the butcher and my store on the corner everything was opening, the Chinese style. During the night you put the bolts in, hook them up from the inside, and this was it. And the third store he was taking in the Chinese barber and there he made a little window and this was a closed store.

So the middle of the store was a butcher and the third store was barbershop. The barber was in that store for about six or eight weeks and he didn't pay any rent. The landlord was coming to me and asked me what he should do. So one think you stay in the store until you take some money and take the money or throw him out. The life in Shanghai is a very funny thing. I will talk this about later. So okay he was giving him shop notice that he was willing to have first of next month willing to have two months rent otherwise he is coming with the police and he is keeping his share and everything was, the tools for the barbershop he will keep till he pays the rent. Two or three days before the end of the month in the morning I was coming to open up my store, the barber was gone. The store was empty. Door was open. He had moved out without paying any rent. (*Manfred chuckles*) Now eh,

Gerda talking with Neil in the background.

Manfred: Now eh, with that store and after I had the whole setup little bit running and it was looking like a little bit money was coming in, we moved from the camp in a private, in a little private room. Now, not that, this was proving my little two wheeler that I had this was very, very good because in the beginning I left my belongings in the store. Then after about three or four months they were breaking in and were taking uh, different cigarettes and other things. From that day on I was wrapping my whole tobacco store in the evening in two big trunks, putting them on my cart, wheeled the whole outfit, that whole tobacco store I wheeled home and the next morning I wheeled the whole thing again to the store. I was decorating fresh and was starting the day over, then in the evening we wrapped everything up and this was the store.

Neil: What were your hours?

Manfred: My hours? My hours at this time, at this time my hours were morning from six to evenings nine to nine-thirty from this time, this time. So, we moved forth and back. We moved forth and back. I will talk about it very, very cute and comical accident what I had, ja an episode. Every morning at five forty-five at same time o'clock I was rolling with my two-wheeler through the lane. I left the Tianshan Road, the lane in Shanghai is the same like in England. This is sixty, eighty to one hundred houses with little side streets and the whole thing is underneath one number, 725, and then each house is got the separate number. So I lived in house 80.

One day I was, I didn't recognize anything special. I was going to the store with my wheeler and the neighbor from the store, there was a big Chinese market there and my neighbor was coming and asking, "What's a matter with you this morning?

You have to know one thing, you are same like an alarm clock for the whole alley. When your little wheeler is wheeling out everybody knows this is five forty-five and everybody was..."

Gerda: The moment you came to the market you noticed...

Manfred: And I was finding out that I was one hour early that day. And then he was coming in my store and he told me, and I didn't know, up until then I didn't know I was the alarm clock for the whole lane. Then he told me, everybody was an hour early this morning because you were an hour early. Your little two wheeler was rolling out an hour earlier and everybody was coming up and everybody was an hour early. (*Manfred chuckles*).

Gerda talking in the background.

Manfred: Ja, there were small family fights because the husband and wife they were fighting husband says, "I have to go" as he is leaving and this must be the time, "No it is an hour earlier." "No, no, fix everything up, I am going because he went." And then I found out this was, the whole thing was an hour early.

I was going on this way for about, with my store, one year. I was going into Shanghai and had my special stores. I wasn't able to buy directly from the cigar factory or cigarette factories because they have to buy in bigger amounts so I made a business that was same like begging. Everybody was able to buy a pack of cigarettes with ten cents at the Chinese store, so he had to pay my store eleven or twelve cents because otherwise I wasn't able to make any profit. This was going on for about a year then the Japanese they were buying houses and houses and houses. And they bought this house where I was living and I had to move. So I moved in my store.

Neil: In back of it?

Manfred: In back of the store.

Neil: Now, wait a minute! Before you go any further, what about the Japanese? What about, they have control of Shanghai when you got there? Or when did they come? Tell about that.

Manfred: Okay, we can set that back and can talk a little bit over the Japanese. In our situation when we were emigrating from Germany, Shanghai was Japanese occupied and this was our luck otherwise the twenty or twenty-five thousand people that were immigrating to Shanghai wasn't able to come in. Would Shanghai not be occupied by Japanese and the original Chinese immigration rules, the Chinese immigration laws would be in order, then we must have had the same formalities. Maybe we were willing to go to America. Maybe we were willing to go to Australia. We were willing to go to someplace else. All the immigration formalities must be settled. Now the Japanese had occupied the Shanghai. They were willing to take everybody in because they were willing to build Shanghai up again. And with the Jewish people, when people were coming in they need housing, and they need living and the Japanese figured they were bringing life and they were bringing rebuilding. And this is what the Jewish people did.

In Hongkou where they were living, whole, nearly sixty percent of Hongkou, the Jewish people, they are rebuilding completely. The houses were all bombed out. So with more Jewish people were coming in they were needing more living quarters. They were living a little bit more business. They were needing a little bit more...they were needing a little bit more housing, and a little bit more living urgencies, and they were needing another barber, and they were needing another shoemaker and another beauty parlor and another, and another, and another. So they were building, the Jewish people were building Hongkou completely new, up. Most, or very many of these people had connections with America and they got help from America with five, or ten, or fifteen dollars a month and this was in Shanghai plenty of money because cost of living when we arrived was very cheap. For one Chinese dollar and $6.40 in Chinese money was one American dollar. So for about one Chinese dollar fifteen American cents, by this time, you were able to buy 100 eggs. You were able to buy six pounds of liver. You were able to buy two chickens. You were able to buy one goose. You were able to buy ten or twelve, fifteen pounds of fish. So for thirty dollars a month you had a complete house for a complete house to rent. For thirty dollars a month or for five American dollars you had an amah [nursemaid] which is the same amount for thirty dollars you had a cookboy, ja cookboy. So cost of living was very cheap and with that money what was coming in from America the Chinese were living good and the Jewish people who got that money, they were making quite a nice living there.

Neil: How did the Japanese treat you? Did you have any trouble with them?

Manfred: In the beginning we didn't have any trouble with the Japanese because they were willing to find cheap labor and this was cheap labor for them because they got that part of Hongkou, this was a suburb from Shanhgai, they got it rebuilt without costing them a penny. So in the beginning they were very, very nice. Still this was very strange, very strange feeling for us because we were Jewish people mostly were going through the concentration camps in Germany. We were living in Shanghai, China, Japanese occupied and the Japanese were partners from Germany. They were partners.

So then coming back to that store where we...then I moved in that store. And uh, we had water, I had water in that store, but no sewer, no toilet, nothing. So when we moved in that store and I lived there then I was willing to make a little bit business with soft drinks and water. Water was the thing in Shanghai when it was distilled, uh (**Gerda**: Filtered.), filtered it was drinking water and this was money for us. So for to open up a store for drinking water you need water and you need a sewer.

So I didn't have any sewer. I bought a little bit like a sink underneath that water pipe, a faucet, underneath the faucet and I made something like a sink around the sink I made something like a curtain. So this was closed. And then when the inspection was coming in from the health department to take the inspection for that drinking business, when I was talking with this inspector, his name was Rahmer. He was coming from the same town I was coming and then we were talking we were going the same school he was living in the same neighborhood I was living in. So, was talking there, and talking there, and talking there the whole thing was all right. I was getting my license from the health department for drinking water. And then my business hours was going a little bit longer.

Gerda: No really, what was underneath, behind that curtain was only a pail.

Manfred: Ja, behind this curtain was no sewer. It was only a pail. For every drop of water what was running over this was running in that pail and three, four or five times a day I had to go out and I'd have to throw the water out and bring it back. Uh, so I got my license and then I had a little bit longer business hours. I had my store open from the morning six to evenings 1:30 a.m. 362 days a year, only three holidays, Rosh Hashanah and Yom Kippur was closed. Otherwise everyday was open. Now at this time the whole situation in Shanghai was getting a little bit worser because we, not we, our Germany, and the second World War was going already. So...

Neil: Yeah, what about when it started now? When the war started in 1939 you were still living in the camp.(**Gerda**: Ja.) (**Manfred**: Ja.) Did you know about that when it started?

Manfred & Gerda: Yes!

Manfred: Ja, we had German papers. We had refugee papers. We were...

Gerda: We had those expe...(**Manfred**: Hmm?) That day you had the accident [Edie's and Gerda's excursion ending with rickshaw accident]

Manfred: We were informed this whole thing was otherwise, for the beginning life was going normal and we, for the beginning we didn't have any change what was, what we were able to fear. Later on this was getting worse and worse and worse.

Neil: Now it was getting worse, yeah. What year now? 1941?

Manfred: This was about 1941, ja. And my daughter was born in 1941.

Neil: Tell about that, a little something.

Manfred: The, eh, she was born in Shanghai and she got the privileges from a Chinese citizen. So I was able to get milk from the city government, canned milk, not fresh milk, canned milk, and very, very cheap because there was already an inflation going. So I was going in once a month to Shanghai , was picking up my milk, was selling the canned milk, was buying fresh milk for her. But this way I was able to afford the fresh milk.

Then after one year they were coming from the government and they were saying very sorry, our stock in milk is out we are not able to give you any canned milk any more because we are out of it. You have to take fresh milk and we will give you and dairy was making daily deliveries to the milk. So I was going out to the dairy one day was inquiring how the whole thing is working and what is supposed to be done. So he told me, the first thing is you have to pay milk for one month ahead of time. And you have to pay a deposit for the bottles for one month, for sixty bottles I guess, for sixty bottles. This was a fortune.

Gerda: I think it was forty or thirty bottles...

Manfred: Thirty bottles. For thirty empty bottles and for one cart of milk daily for a month ahead of time to pay, this was a fortune. Now with my very, very short stock of money what I had, because I was very poor, this was impossible for me to put that money down for one month ahead of time to get the milk. So I had neighbors, very good neighbors, and I was borrowing $100 from one neighbor and $100 from another. This was in grocery store and I was putting down that deposit for one month's money for the milk and I got this going. Then later on I had to, from every dollar or fifty cents or two I earned I was paying back what I owed them. And this was going on, was coming and going, I borrowed $100 and paid it back, and borrowed another $100 and paid it back because now.

Shortly here I like to go in for the money what I made in Colombo. It's this amount of money with fifteen, with nine English pounds and twelve American dollars I opened up my store. That was all of my money I had. So I need a little bit and few shelves, and I need a little bit table and I need a little bit there, and I need a little bit sign outside. So I was very, very short on money. I was sitting there and I was figuring when I'm buying three cartons of cigarettes I'm able to earn a $1.50 and I'm buying for that same amount of money I'm buying cigars. I would be able to earn three dollars only the cigarettes are turned over in two days. In two days I have that $1.50 profit. That box of cigars was three dollars that was standing there for maybe five, six, eight or ten days so eh, I had to buy very, very careful that I had everything what was asking for and still to have in good supply and different kinds of cigars and different kinds of cigarettes.

Now I'm willing to come back to that drinking business. The situation where water and the whole thing was rationed. We had rationed power and we had rationed water. Power I had in electric cooker, only one flame. So this was pretty good and that was rationed and, quite fair prices over there, was the cheapest thing to cook. And water we had a special amount of water what we were able to use. I didn't use one drop of water from my own water faucet. I was using that only for drinking water. I paid for myself, for every little bit of water what I was using privately, for washing the baby clothes, for cooking. Next to my store was a Chinese market and the coolies there they had water because they had to clean the asphalt and the market stalls. So I paid them I think $300 a month, $300 Chinese dollars a month and I was able to go over with buckets and I was bringing in my own water what I was using for myself, cooking and washing and cleaning. This I paid for privately.

Now is coming in very, very bad episode because I was getting sick. I catched dysentery and I was going to the doctor and I was getting pills and the whole thing was after one and a half weeks, the whole thing was...everybody was thinking healed and from then on in intervals, I was sick. Once I had amoebic dysentery and once I had lumbaling and this is more technical. There were healing one. One [type of] dysentery they were healing and the other one was still there. Then the other one was breaking out and they were healing this and then the amoebic is there again. This was going on for about 3 1/2 or 4 years. Where I had my store and where I lived I don't have any toilet. I had to go to the Ward Road *Heim*. There they had the facilities. It was about two and a half blocks. With my dysentery some times, some day I had to go a hundred times and I was running to the camp and I was just making it and I was coming back I was tired and poofed. I was just sitting, willing to sit down for five minutes and there I had to go again.

This was going on for about three years. All the examinations, there was a few times in Shanghai hospital and I was fighting for the medicine. And eh, coming and going. I borrowed more money and I paid back more money. I was arranging and I was, and only now I don't like to give wrong impression. I have to give one episode what really happened what was very, very interesting. When I was laying down with my dysentery the first day and Chinese guy, we had the little Chinese stoves. They call it flower pot with charcoal and we were doing some relief cooking besides our electric plate. And this day I was laying down the first day a Chinese guy was reaching into the boards and was taking a water kettle, this hot water away, stealing.

The same day and later in the day a person was coming and was asking for me and I was coming up and he said, "I am from Tianshan and refugee too and we are needing plenty of cigarettes because in Tianshan the cigarettes are more expensive than in Shanghai" Black market, was that...? I would be able to buy for him a hundred box of cigarettes. Fulhaus was his name. Yeah I can do it. So the first day, was the first business in the evening I told him I can make that business with you. I don't have such big amount of money. You should give me that money in advance and in the evening you can have the cigarettes and I was taking a small profit on it. He said this is all right, I trust you.

So we made the first business this way and I earned exactly that kettle what they were stealing in the afternoon from my stove I was exactly earning the same amount of money what that kettle was and I bought that kettle back and from this day on this person from Tianshan he was doing with me business, doing all my time I was ill and all the money I was spending for my illness I earned on him. And the moment I was well again he wasn't coming anymore. Just opposite the last business I made with him he was a little bit short on money and I thought take a few boxes more and I paid for it and he did and then he wasn't coming back. So this is very, very interesting episode.

Now eh, with my illness coming and going, now my daughter was very sick. She got dysentery too and she was losing, or she was without any salt in her body and without any fluid.

Neil: How old was she?

Manfred: A year and a half. She was in doctor's care and she was getting salt injections and one of these injections infected her. She got an infection from this and she was very, very sick. So one day we were with her the whole night. She couldn't sleep and she was crying and she was in pain and she was really quite sick. She was really quite sick but Dr. Glass examined her then he told me, "Listen, I would be you, I would try to get your daughter in the hospital."

Neil: Where was this doctor?

Manfred: Dr. Glass.

Neil: In the French Town?

Manfred: In the French town. An immigrant doctor he was since 1933 in Shanghai. So he said I have a way maybe able to, can fix this. There is a general hospital where all German speaking personnel is from Switzerland or somehow. He says, "Before I was working with that hospital, but not anymore now. So I am giving you a slip that this hospital should take your daughter for free bed of my name and then find out what is going on. I'm telling you now when you are coming in that hospital don't give that slip. First ask is there a bed, if they have a bed for you." Okay. Then I ask him how much I owe you for the examination and he said, "You know nothing. Your kid is really quite sick so when you have a little bit money spend it on her."

So from there I went to this hospital and there was a bed free and then I showed them my slip and the nurse said to me, "You know that's very sorry you can't have that bed. We don't work any more with Dr. Glass. Your committee has free beds. In Hongkou you have the committee from the Jewish Welfare Board and there are beds and they should give you a slip and the whole thing is okay." So there was a Dr. Holliford [who] was a customer of mine in my little tobacco store and he was in charge for the slips for that.

Neil: We'll continue on the next roll. Tell them!

Manfred: We'll continue on the next roll.

Disc Three-Side Two

Manfred: End of the first session.

Neil: This whole part.

Manfred: This whole part. So, then I was going back to Hongkou after. In that hospital I had the guarantee that the bed would be for me. 'Til three o'clock this afternoon, they would keep it for me. I went back to Hongkou and I was trying to reach Dr. Holliford. He was the director of this part from the Jewish Welfare Fund what was in charge for that general hospital in Shanghai. So I reached him in the house of a good friend of his, Dr. Deutsch and I talked to him and he said to me, "Ja, this needs time. There is not a chance that you have your daughter today afternoon, (**Gerda**: Saturday afternoon), Saturday afternoon and that we have to hold inquiries, your belongings, investigation. Maybe you are able to pay for yourself. We don't know what you have for money. So I told him Doctor, I have an old typewriter here, and I have an old pair of shoes and I have one extra suit for myself and I have a little bit these things. Keep it and you give me that. No, it isn't so easy.

So we, he told me, were fighting and we were discussing and we were discussing then in our discussion I can give you, I can bring your daughter in the Chinese hospital and you can have this to sedate her. Dr. Glass told me nothing, don't take in Chinese hospital. For this case it's general hospital very good and try to get her in. Now we can do it but you will have to wait at least middle of next week but forbidden by this time my daughter is gone, she's dead because she is very sick. I'm sorry I can't help you.

Now the last minute, eh, I was getting an idea and I was willing to try the following things. A neighbor of mine Mr. Natowitz, he had a son. He was quite sick and he was in the same hospital and he was needing blood transfusion and one day, we were very good friends, one day I told him, you know Mr. Natowitz, in case Yoshi, that was his name, Yoshi needs next time some blood, I'm willing to give some for him. Oh, that's very nice. That's very kind and you go in that same general hospital and blood center and get your blood type and then the next time the situation is coming up we will call on you. The next situation was coming up. They were calling on me. It was too late. So I wasn't able to give any blood for him anymore because he died. He passed away.

So this was my idea. So now I know my blood group and then I was asking [the] director, "Doctor I have a question to you, there are not times a situation coming up where you need some blood for people there under your care." "Oh, ja he says, yes, for blood we are always interested." "So I'm making you an offer now. You give me that slip that I'm able to get my daughter today afternoon in this hospital. And I'm guarantee you so much and so plenty blood that you are willing to have you get free of charge from me when you give me that slip." "Okay", he says, ""I'm sitting down and I'm writing. And I got my daughter in the hospital. And after three and a half weeks she was coming out perfectly all right and thank God there is nothing left over from that.

So um, eh, there are so, so plenty such stories. There are so plenty things we lived through and when I am trying to get the whole thing in order and when I'm trying to give the whole idea, the right picture I'm sorry to say sometimes things are slipping away because there is one episode and on this episode there is another one and uh so you are getting sometimes probably carried away. And that's end of part five.

Session number six.

Manfred: Today I am willing to talk about life in Shanghai and little episodes what happened to me there. So I'm willing to begin with a friend of mine. He passed away and we were going to his funeral and on our way back, and we were completely dressed and we had hats and on our way back in a streetcar, open windows because Shanghai was quite hot and humid so windows were always open. On the stop, when Chinese was passing by grabbing, reaching in through that open window to my hat and was running away. So my hat was gone. So we stop. I was jumping out of the streetcar was running behind this Chinese guy. I was running, I was running and then we were coming to an alley. No sign of the Chinese and no sign of my hat. This was life in Shanghai. Stealing in Shanghai isn't against the law. Against the law in Shanghai and China is when you are able to catch somebody. Somebody is caught in the act of stealing, that's against the law and he is completely guilty and everybody who is catching one person stealing is completely up to him what he is willing to do. Other episodes, I had my store and one evening behind that fruit and meat market, green vegetables, fruit and meat, was a big opening houses completely down and no rebuilt. It was completely...

Neil: Rubble?

Manfred: Rubbish?

Neil: Rubble.

Manfred: Rubble, rubble ja. So one day in the late afternoon I had a little bit soft drinks. A few persons were there and had a drink and one Chinese was coming up and was stealing from one of my customers a hat. And then he was running out that rubbish through, as a street, Morit Road. I was running behind him and the Morit Road I got him. I catched him. And I was bringing him right away to the police station there and the officer was taking everything to protocol and he told me no, this is very nice, such resolute people like you. We should have more then crime wouldn't be so high. Then he told me next morning there is a court hearing and that guy is coming for court and I should be there at 10 o'clock. I should be in the police station at 10 o'clock. So next morning at 10 o'clock I was at police station, and we were taking with the, black maria, police cars, black maria. How do they call it here?

Gerda: What?

Manfred: No, no the car where they are transporting the prisoner? Black maria.

Neil: Oh yeah, the eh, police wagon.

Manfred: Police wagon. So we were going to court with the police wagon then there was court session and I got to person who talking German and Chinese and I was telling the story in German and the other person was translating to the judge the story in Chinese and then he was sentenced to jail for sixty days. And I was able to get that hat for my customer back. I had to pay a little bit commission, what do they call it, tips, and the whole thing was finished.

That's another thing. I had this little two-wheeler car and one day a Chinese police sergeant, "You have such a cart?"

"Ja."

"You have a license for that cart?"

"Ja sure I have a license."

"Can I see it?"

"What the license?"

"No, the cart."

Okay we standing outside before the door and he said no there is not such a cart and I was looking and no there was not such a cart. So then he told me you better...

Gerda: No...

Manfred: Probably my neighbor, sometimes when he has plenty to live on he has three such carts and he is short and come up and he is taking mine and he is doing deliveries with it. So I was going over to him and I was asking there. "No we don't have your cart." But then he was coming out and he told me, your cart is stolen. This is a standing on the police station, you better come with me there are some formalities. Okay so I was taking rickshaw with him and we were going to the police station. So there the officer was taking the protocol really he got different questions for me.

"You have a license?"

"Yes."

"You the owner of the truck?"

"Ja."

"How much is it worth?" he says.

"Oh, about five hundred, six hundred dollars, Chinese dollars, 1,000 dollars."

Okay he's writing down 1,000 dollars. Then he was telling, he told me the story from the police. That guy who stole that little two-wheeler he was going in the shop where they are making such carts and he was willing to sell it. He [the shop owner] was informing the police and so once this, so was coming my little two-wheeler to the station. So he says, the next morning you are coming here eleven o'clock, eleven-thirty it's at court because you have to tell your story again.

So I was there and same procedure with that hat. I was taking the stand. There was a guy he was talking, I was telling the story in German and he translated it in English and in Chinese and then he told me same story. That guy is getting sixty days and now you can come, no now we don't take a rickshaw, now we are walking to the police station. And on the way to the police station so he was coming now and told me. "This is the way this is going here in Shanghai. We are going now to the station and you"...What's that?

Talking in background.

Manfred: Eh, now we were walking to the station and he told me that whole police system is filled up in informer money. So when they are catching somebody they have to ask for money because they have to pay for their informers. He says, "Your cart is probably worth 1,000 dollars and we are handling such kinds of business. You pay 500 dollars and then you pick up your cart." So I was starting in the business. I was always short on money and I wasn't able and willing to pay 500 dollars. So I told him, "When you are willing to have 500 dollars from me forget the whole thing. You keep that cart and that's it because I don't have 500 dollars to pay for that cart." They wanted to know what I would be able to pay, so listen, "I'm just starting out in business and I'm partly living on relief and I don't have any money at all and I have a young child." And then he said to me, "Now you have to see our side of the story too. We have to pay our informers otherwise we aren't able to keep order here in town and what are you willing to pay?"

And now listen, "Let me tell you something. I'm willing, not I'm willing to get around this, the whole thing I am willing to pay you 100, 100 Chinese dollars. Take it or leave it. That's it. You take it, all right I take my cart. You don't take it, I leave my cart, that's it." Now he isn't able to make decision because there are guys above him who were making the decisions. I should come at least the next morning to the station, should have the 100 dollars along and then he will, then he will let me know I am able to take my cart or they're not willing to make this kind of business for 100 dollars to give me my little two wheeler back. So I was going home and I was quite mad. I was asking myself, who is supposed to get sixty days? That Chinese guy who was stealing my car or the police who were willing to take 500 dollars for that? I am getting my property back.

So the next morning I went to the station with my 100 dollars and uh, he was waiting, he said be there ten o'clock and I am usually very much on time. So I was there at ten o'clock and he was waiting at the entrance already and he said to me, "I think you have good luck. You give me that 100 dollars and I am going in willing to give the boss that 100 dollars and when he is taking it then I am coming out and I am nodding my head and you can take the little two wheeler and go away." He was going in. He was coming out again nodding his head. The whole thing was over. And there are plenty of such stories...

Neil talking in background.

Manfred: Ja. Then the American flyers were coming like the watch over Shanghai I think from Okinawa they were coming and bombing the outskirts from Shanghai because the Japanese had their munitions and information centers and telephone and radio what was communication centers and so. They were coming like twice, in the morning and the evening they were coming and bombing at outskirts. So on the corner, we were in the ordered blackouts. We were always in blackouts. And across, when the alarm was ringing everybody has to be black.

And across my, on the corner of that market hall was a big street lamp up and one day that bulb was burnt out. So I was willing to have that fixed because on that bulb, in the evening I was making my little business, my little soft drinks. So I was inquiring at the coolies from the market hall and they told me, okay they will inform the guys and they were coming and they are fixing it. So they were coming with that truck and with the big ladders and with the bulb and then they were coming at my store and they were asking me,

"Uh, you were complaining about that bulb?"

"No, not directly complaining only I was willing to find out who was supposed to fix that."

"Oh we're supposed to fix that."

"Okay, then go ahead and fix it."

"No, this isn't going so fast. We can't fix it right away. What are you willing to pay for that?"

"I myself willing to pay for that? I myself not willing to pay a penny for that."

"No then we are going and we are leaving it."

"And okay you go and leave it. But I am telling you something now. I have a very good friend in the city government, so I will talk to them and you will see that you're in trouble. What is that? What kind of business? You get paid for that and then when you are making something you are willing to squeeze some money out of me. You don't get a penny out of me. Fix it, that's okay. Don't fix it, you come back two or three days later and I will show you how that is done."

So they were going crossing the street, going in a huddle, talking things over and then they were raising up the ladder and then were fixing that bulb. So I was coming around this business without paying anything and China is nothing down before. There [it] is very, very known what *kumsha*, tips, this nothing done without tips.

We had in that little store we had was a friend of ours. He was making business with leather. And he was going always to Shanghai at the town and was bringing home the leather in the rickshaw and this was a fortune for Shanghai. When he was in the rickshaw and he had the leather ahead of him it was quite, quite very expensive stuff he was carrying.

Neil: Leather for shoes?

Manfred: Ja, sole leather. Shoes, ja. And one day he was coming home, he was out a hat. What's happened? Oh, I was in trouble today. Why? So I was traveling along nice and quietly, just out of nowhere a guy was grabbing my hat, was running away. What should I do? I had maybe fifty or sixty thousand Shanghai dollars leather in front of me. This hat was maybe worth sixty, eighty or a hundred dollars worth, lots of money for me. What should I do? I was leaving him run only to protect my leather because they were thinking I was making one mistake by stopping the rickshaw and was running for my hat there was my leather gone.

So this is life in Shanghai. Otherwise life everything in Shanghai is taking place on the streets. I think I don't have to talk about it because this is a very, very much known factor. You have the little dinettes where they are carrying stove and the bumpers. They are carrying on one side the stove and on the other side the food and in little compartments underneath dishes and the chopsticks. The barber is going the same way. They are carrying shoes, Chinese shoes, and all kinds of business laying open on the street. It's just completely in business matter an open town. You have the little stores and you have the walking around stores.

I am coming to, I think, a very serious matter in my Shanghai life. We had, I had a store on Chusan Road across the market, across the green market and across that big Shanghai prison. And that prison, where a big wall, this was fixed up like in concentration camp. Wall was maybe two or three floors high and two or three blocks, figured for here, two or three blocks. On the corners and in the middle this big outlooks where they were able to see what's going on. And inside and a little bit to our left far up the third or fourth floor was same thing like in, not a tower, but same thing in back alley, and there they were walking, the prisoners, I think there were prisoners in for life and for...

Neil: War. POW's?

Manfred: Ja. POWs, and robbers, and murderers. There was everything in that prison. This was a very, very big outfit. This was a square of three or four American city blocks square and high, six, seven stories high. So one night we were sitting outside and watchmen from the warehouse was there and other of our friend was there and out of nowhere was coming down, they're coming down bedsheets, putting one to another, just figured out this was reaching the wall down to the street and there they were coming up, six or seven guy crossing the street and were going running in opposite directions and were gone.

Fifteen or twenty minutes later the lights were going on big. The alarm bells were ringing. Everybody was running at the streets. The Japanese Bridge guard, this is so same like FBI here or Gestapo in Germany. No, this is not a comparison, Gestapo in Germany, let's put it this way, and the Russian Secret Service and very, very political outfit. They were coming were closing the corners on all the bridges they were going out Chusan Road Bridge and Garden Bridge what's going into Shanghai. The whole thing was blocked with military personnel and then friends that were there they were telling me, "You close your door. You go in and you stop and go all the way in. Otherwise you will be in trouble. There will be going on, will be a big investigation, and maybe you're in trouble".

Okay I close my store and from the inside actually we had a window in there and we were looking out and they were lighting one special cell. This is, later on we were find out this is the cell where the prisoners were living in and they were escaping and then we find out this were American flyers

Neil: How many were there?

Manfred: Six or seven I guess they escaped and the way I heard it two made it and the other they catched. The whole thing must be really figured out and later on we find out the whole. The prisoner guards were on strike. And uh, this was quite an exciting moment when we saw that.

TAPE STOPS

Manfred: When the refugees, the Jewish people arrived in Shanghai in groups. In between let's say one, one, one and half years, few or quite a part they were getting settled and they were living in French town and in settlement. Then in 1943 the Japanese were willing to put, same like the Germans, same like the Jews, same like in the Ghetto. They called it designated area. So everybody who was living outside this area had got special, got the time limit and they had to move in that area. They were giving up their little bit business what they were. Business was they had in French town and the settlements and were moving in the designating area.

Neil: You had to move too?

Manfred: No, we lived, we don't have to move because we lived in that part in Hongkou what was designating area. Then the Japanese were coming up with special passes. Little business, little store keeper or business men, they are suppose to buy their goods for they were needing for their stores they had to go to Shanghai. They got special passes. There was a guy, his name was Ghoya. They called him the King of the Jews. He was quite... seemed like a tyrant. Every month you have to apply anew for your passport that you were able to leave the designating area...

Neil: Pass, not passport.

Manfred: No pass, ja, pass, for a pass. There you have to stand in time, for three, four, five, six hours and when you were coming up to go, ja, you had, he had always different kinds of questions to you. Then he was in good moods you have no trouble at all, you get your pass. When he was not so good moods you had to come back three, four, five times before you get it. You get slapped and this was terrible time. This was 1943.

Neil: Now this is the most important historical part, right?

Manfred: Ja. Now is coming I think very, the most important historical part for the lives, from the Jewish people in Shanghai. They were opening up stores. Grocery stores, one or two in our district in the designating area that you were able to buy there. They were giving goods a little bit cheaper than other stores. You have to file applications, register in it. The registration we find out later was the same thing that the registrations when the Jewish people were sent to the gas chambers in Europe. How many gold teeth and uh...[Data was collected when they registered Jews in the community. Everyone had to register. People had to register, background, property and then that was confiscated and used against the Jews]

Gerda: Well the registration was maybe four or five pages.

Neil: To fill out?

Manfred: Ja, the registration four or five pages, to fill out. How many gold teeth and all such questions and eh...What color hair? And how high? And what for marks?

Gerda: How many operations you had! Think of it!

Manfred: How many operations you had?

Neil: Just very personal.

Manfred: Very personal registration. And then later on we heard and it was all talking about it, that the gas chambers in Shanghai were ready on an island in the Yangtze River and the Germans were willing to take the Jewish people to the gas chambers. The Japanese government wasn't willing. The emperor wasn't willing to go along.

Neil: Did you see these chambers?

Manfred: We didn't saw the chambers because we couldn't get out of our district.

Neil: They were ready. How did you know they were ready? What proof? Really, what proof?

Manfred: Proof. There isn't direct proof. People were there and they told us they saw it on that islands. And eh, they saw it on that island and I myself believe it because when I am thinking back at the registration we did at the grocery store, so there was something to it. And very, very...

Gerda: This came out later that emperor wasn't willing to go along.

Manfred: Ja, the talks between the German government and the Japanese government were going on. The emperor wasn't willing to go along. (**Gerda**: This was late in '45-*continues talking*) This was late in '45. This was shortly before the war was over. I think the American authorities will have some proof for that because I think they found gas chambers on the island in Shanghai. [As of 2013 no evidence has come to light confirming gas chambers on the island; however, it is important to understand that whether or not the gas chamber existed, those in the Ghetto were unable to confirm or deny.]

Now I'm willing to talk about one very terrifying noon hour.

Terrifying noon hour- I was sick with my dysentery again and I was coming out of hospital and I had a special diet. So they had for refugees set up special kitchens, diet kitchens. And for my daughter she got children's food, there was an extra kitchen. So, on this day, on this day it must be already 1945, I guess. It's very late, very late.

Gerda: July 17th, 1945.

Manfred: July 17th, 1945 it was. Eh, very cloudy day. The clouds were hanging very deep. My late father-in-law he was going to the Kinchow Road kitchen for my daughter's food and I myself was going in the diet kitchen in Tianshan Road and we were both out and the sirens were sounding. And when I was passing in Tianshan Road in that kitchen alley in the main entrance I heard the sounds of the planes flying over, quite deep [low]. And then there was a direct bombardment. This was maybe going on for 6 or 8 seconds and they left again. Half of that immigration went down, they were hitting really this immigration center fell down.

So I was running home, was rushing home. I lost one shoe on my way home and I was just coming home. My wife and my daughter they were alone, they were in that store, far in a corner. My daughter she was crying. My wife was crying. One and half blocks a way a big warehouse was hit. This was in flames. Then we were worried about my late father-in-law. Then he was coming a half an hour later and then the news were coming in. One of those big refugee camps, I think this was Tianshan Road or Ward Road, I don't know, sure of the name now. That was next to that home was Japanese communication center and they were willing to hit this and there they were knocking out completely that communication center and they were hitting that camp. And the houses around Tianshan Road there was down and plenty of casualties. I think 17 Jews.

Gerda: No, 37...

Manfred: Oh, 37 Jews killed in that whole bombardment and they were digging, all the houses were falling together, and they were digging for one and a half, two weeks before the whole thing was cleared. Hundreds and hundreds and hundreds of Chinese died in that bombardment and everything was closed so I had drinking water. They were coming through Chusan Road, by my store, with the dead people, they were carrying and...

Gerda: Injured...

Manfred: And the injured, mainly the injured and the dead people they were bringing them to hospitals and the people that were digging, I had the drinking water out on the street, everybody that was passing and was working you had a free drink and I had cigarettes there for the workers. This was terrible, terrible thing.

Neil: How about more bombings? Any more bombings?

Manfred: That was the only direct bombing of that refugee center.

Neil: Were their other bombings?

Manfred: Ja! Around, around the harbor the Bund, and around the outskirts for the Japanese. The Japanese had all the munition centers. One night they were hitting and the munition storage place. The whole night the explosion were going up one after another. Every fifteen or twenty minutes another explosion.

Gerda: Every available Jew was helping.

Manfred: Every available and healthy Jew was helping digging and was clearing debris to find dead people or injured ones. (**Gerda**: You couldn't.) I wasn't able to go along because I just got out of hospital and I was still sick. So I was standing on the street and I was helping with water and with refreshments. And I think this was my terrible experience what I had while in Shanghai.

Now eh, in very, very sad experience I had one Christmas. We lived, my wife, my father-in-law, myself, and my daughter. She was born in Shanghai. We lived together.

Neil: In one room?

Manfred: Ja, my daughter, my wife and myself, we were living in one room and my father-in-law he lived in a camp, in a refugee camp. He slept in a camp but he was all day with us together. One, for Christmas we were getting from the refugee committee for the kids, for my daughter, I was getting 40,000 Shanghai dollar. This was a time where the inflation was really quite high and money wasn't too much worth anymore.

Gerda: That was in 1944

Manfred: Ja, I think 1944. This was quite an unusually cold Christmas time in Shanghai because all the nine and a half years we lived in Shanghai I saw only once a little bit snow. This little bit snow was too much for Chinese people. They were dying on the streets. Oh, thousand over thousands people died in one night in Shanghai on the streets. So my daughter, she was not quite well. She was a little bit sick and she was very cold and she was standing in her bed and she was crying. She wasn't feeling good and she was cold. So I decided to go and buy some wood. We had a stove in our room. We never used it. (**Gerda**: Little iron stove.) Little iron stove, very little. In German they call it, *Kanonenofen*. I don't know how this is called here. I don't think such an oven is here. Very, very small, wood burner or maybe bit coal. So I bought for the 40,000 dollars I was going out and bought wood and I was making fire in that stove.

Neil: How much wood did you get for 40,000 dollars?

Manfred: Oh maybe fifty pounds wood. Fifty pounds of wood or maybe forty pounds of wood, (**Neil**: 40,000 dollars?) Ja, 40,000 dollars. And I was making a fire and I could see myself, how my daughter was feeling better. She was warming up. She laughed and she start playing. And I was burning that 40,000 dollar wood right away in the room. And then it was maybe two hours or three hours and then that stove was getting cold and the room was getting cold again too because that was only boards and the wind was coming in and much air was coming in, so there wasn't any protection at all.

After that fire was gone for one hour, my daughter was starting again to cry and to feel uncomfortable and unsatisfactor... (**Gerda**: Unsatisfied) unsatisfied. So what I was doing, she was getting 40,000 dollars from the committee as a Christmas present. I was going in my own pocket and was taking out 40,000 dollars, was going buying the same amount of wood, was coming back making a fire and my daughter was thawing off again and after the fire was going for twenty to twenty-five minutes she was playing. She was laughing and she was feeling satisfied. And...

Gerda: This way she had it warm one whole afternoon.

Manfred: One whole afternoon we had it warm and this was costing me 40,000 dollars. (*Manfred chuckles*) All right. 40,000 dollars. 40,000 from the committee and 40,000 dollars from myself.

Neil: So, eighty.

Manfred: So 80,000 dollars, ja.

Neil: For one afternoon.

Manfred: Ja. Now another very, very nice episode to tell and this is the night the news was coming through, the war is over. The news was hitting us. I had that store closed already at about, oh let's say, this time I didn't have so long office hours anymore...

Neil: Well, now did you know about the war in Europe? Or did you know about the whole war?

Manfred: Ja, the whole war. We knew everything. We had newspapers and we were...

Neil: You knew Europe was in the war.

Manfred: Ja, we knew Europe was in the war and we knew Japan was in it. We know that.

Neil: You knew the Hiroshima bomb?

Manfred: Ja. And then the news was coming through, the war is over. Strange people on the road they were falling on each other...

Gerda: All along it was quiet and then the musicians came back from ...

Manfred: So we had our store closed already and the musicians they were playing, they were making music in the settlement. They were coming back and were bringing the news the war is over. And this was spreading around like...I don't know...

Neil: Wildfire.

Manfred: Ja, like, and shortly after that everybody knew that and so then I opened up my little store a little bit again because people told me "Open up!" Everybody is willing to celebrate a little bit what they've got for money. So was willing to celebrate, smoking a good cigar or having a drink.

Neil: Great, people kissing each other?

Gerda: Sailors.

Manfred: Ja, people on the street were falling each other in the arms, were kissing one another, strangers and eh, embracing it and jumping around, were dancing in the streets, wild.

Gerda: The groups came marching. Whole columns just came marching.

Manfred: Ja, whole columns were marching through from the camps, through the streets and there was quite, till late night, there was big celebration going on. Then the young Jewish people were taking over the police station and were going around and were tearing down the signs from the designating area. And then we went to bed and the next morning first time (*muffled voices*) everybody was told this isn't true. The war isn't over. The Japanese didn't surrender and this is all going on. And then the same day late in the afternoon the real, eh, news was coming through the war was over.

Neil: So, was it really a day early that you found out?

Manfred: No the war was over right. The authorities were willing to give out apology right away and then they told us this isn't so and the same day afternoon this was all right.

Now from this day on, from the business matter went just the opposite way. Shanghai was in inflation. This was never good to have money for long time in your house because wasn't anything and you were losing when you had laying money down too long you lost. In this evening when the news were coming through the war is over I made quite little bit cash that night. So on the next morning I was willing to go all way out and find something big for that, cigars and cigarettes. I had a terrible time to find something. Nobody was willing to take that money anymore. Nobody was willing to take that money anymore. And then two or three weeks later it was very good to hold a little bit money in your belongings because for goods, you were paying today, let's name a figure, 50,000 dollars, you were able to buy that two days later for 35,000 and you were able to buy that another two days later for 28,000. So it was very good to sell your old stock and keep some money that you make some profit out of it. This was such an unusual time. It was such a mix up. Nobody was knowing anymore really what was going on.

From now on our (*Gerda in background talking.*) Now I'm willing to describe in very, very big power showing what the allies were showing after the war was over. Three or four weeks after the war was over the whole Far East fleet, the whole Far East fleet was coming into Shanghai Harbor and thousand over thousands and thousand over thousands more of planes were flying over town in waves. One thousand that wave was going. Another thousand were coming and another thousand were coming and the G.I.s were coming into Shanghai and there was a power showing tremendous. And from,

Neil: What did you after the war was over and you when got out? You still had the store and you ran it, right? You still opened your store.

Manfred: Ja, I opened my store and then life was getting a little bit better and easier for us and then the UNRRA [United Nations Relief and Rehabilitation Administration] was coming in and we were getting UNRRA rations. We were getting food what we didn't have for years. And we don't have to pay for it. And C-rations and 10-in-1 and K-rations and coffee. Before we were able to buy a half ounce of coffee and then from when UNRRA rations were coming in we were getting every month a pound of coffee per person. So things we get American cigarettes from, with the rations, and we get butter and we got meat and we got all plenty very, very good canned stuff. So from there on was our intention to go out to reach normal life so fast as possible.

Manfred: Which was left by the time we didn't know what

was left and eh...Then German Jewish people in *Soufbrau*. They were starting to bring in their papers, lists from survivors from *Auschwitz*, from survivors from *Sachsenhausen*, from survivors from Treblinka.

Neil: You had family there.

Manfred: I had a brother in *Auschwitz*. I had my parents in *Theresienstadt*. Nobody survived. I had a sister with my brother-in-law and a nephew. They were near Warsaw. And then they were in Warsaw Ghetto and they were fighting there and were killed in Warsaw. So this, all things we had to find out by and by. We were writing the Red Cross and we were writing to the *Hofbräu* and we were writing to all the information centers. We were writing to *Theresienstadt* and so by and by we got all that very sad information. I am the last one from my family who survived.

Now uh, then Jews were coming through, people were able to go back to Germany or were able to go as displaced persons to America. So we decided we're not willing to go back to Germany. So we decided to go to America. I had a cousin of my wife, he was living in Milwaukee, Wisconsin and he was sending us affadavits and then we got a call to the American Consulate in Shanghai and then we find out that the affadavit it was strong enough and then I applied for corporate affadavit through the Jewish Organizations and I got this and then I was starting to sell out my little store, my cigars, my cigarettes, what I had.

And then we were waiting to come out. My wife she got, little bit, she got little bit, how should I say, an examinations for that American Consulate. She got shadows on her lung so I had to wait year before (*Gerda talking*). Ja, two months set back and before the next time we were before the consulate again that was about a year. And shortly before we got the second call for that consulate for doctor examinations for the x-rays we had to bring along, my daughter, she got a little bit (**Gerda**: Pneumonia), pneumonia. And then we made x-rays and that, that guy who made x-rays. "There is nothing shows on that x-ray. You shouldn't have any problems with your daughter. And your wife should be all right too." Then we went again to the German consul, to the American Consulate for the examinations. My picture he looked at and he said, "Yeah okay." My wife's picture he said, "This is all right too." I was falling something down from chest. And then he was looking down at my daughter's x-rays and then he says nothing. And then he said, "What are you waiting for? You going in. You have to get undressed. You have little bit more examinations." I was scared. I was scared stiff. I was scared to ask him what's about my daughter so I was going into that room and next to this was only partitions. One room was for the boys, for the men, and one was for the women. And there somebody was knocking on that wall and said,

"Eh, you in there?"

"Ja. I'm all right, I know that."

"What is with our daughter?"

"Oh, she is all right too."

So then finally in 194...(**Gerda**: Eight), 1948, on February, February 17th. On 17h of February we left Shanghai only with the very sad result that we had to left behind my late father-in-law. He got that very unlucky Polish quota and he had to wait.

End of session six.

Session seven.

Manfred: Now I'm willing to fill in some minor accidents, (**Neil**: Incidents) incidents what I think are very cute and they are fitting in the whole story.

Pick pocket, stealing in China isn't against the law. Against the law is when somebody is there and is catching you. This is against the law. Pick pocket is a very profitable business and is partly done under watch, or was partly done, let's put it this way, under watch or in connection with police protection. And across my street, I mentioned it...was a big market, green market and meat market, and there was a gang of boys, 17, 18 years of age. Six or seven and in the morning hours when the market was open there was lots of people movement there. So they were going along the people, were taking, two were taking one person in the middle, and eh, picking his pocket and away they go. Three, four people, next set and doing the same thing. So they were making lots of money in the mornings there. Under police protection when somebody was hollering and going to policeman, that he is willing to do something and nothing was done.

So one day before my store, my late father-in-law, he was outside and we knew the guys, I know the guys all. One of the fellows was coming, my father-in-law was on that little two-wheeler and was putting something on and he was coming and he was willing to steal something from me. Then I was going out and I told him, "Listen, when you are stealing out there, this is none of my business. This is my father-in-law. Those are my belongings. In case you are willing to steal here, I break all your necks what you got on you. I don't need any police protection in this case. I take all of you together and I think you better stay out. Otherwise I am willing to form here another gang and we are watching you and you get what's coming to you. From this day on, they never tried in to steal something from my wife, from my father-in-law, and from me. It was like a protection. They were scared. It was the only way to go against it.

After I had my store for about two or three months, a Chinese boy, age maybe 12, 13 years of age, he was coming and the way we were able to understand each other, he had a bag in his hand and he was willing to, I'm taking that bag in and keep it for him and he got something to do and that bag was in his way. All right put it in and I am watching it for you. Okay. After three hours he was coming back, was willing to pick up his bag. After he got his bag back he was opening it up and was starting to holler and to cry. I couldn't understand anything and hollering and crying and crying and hollering. So I was going to my neighbor, a very educated, eh, Chinese and eh, he was coming over. I told him please would you come over and help me, I eh, there is some trouble and I don't know what's going on and then he was coming over and then he was talking with that boy and then he told me, "You made a big mistake. This is a thing you should learn, never take something for storage in your store, because this a very, very old pitch and bob. They are taking something, storing something in your store, and when they are coming back then they are telling you, you are stealing something out of it. You're not able to prove that."

And there were lots of people standing before my open store and they were watching what was going on and they were listening to that little boy, twelve-year-old boy, and I was quite in trouble there. So one of my friends was coming along so I was sending him right away over to the police station. This was one and a half blocks away and policeman was coming and I told him what was going on and he was taking that little boy and myself into the police station with that bag of bread was it. So then the police officer there, these were all German guys, so they were asking me, they know me already because I was a few times in that police station, they were asking me, what's my trouble and I told them. This little boy was coming and begging me I should take his bag in and I should keep it for two or three hours and then he was coming back and I would have stolen two or three breads out of his pack. Ridiculous, I said. But then they were questioning that little boy and he was telling nearly about the same story only when he was getting his bag back he was coming, it was looking to him like this was small and I was taking two or three breads out of his bag. Then they were putting him in chain and they were chaining him against the wall, that little boy, and then they were asking him again and he was telling the same story and then they were whipping him. And then he told them, no I didn't steal anything and he made it up because he was willing to make two or three breads. His family is sick and all those stories on to it. Oh okay, I was able to go and they keeped him in custody. I don't know what they did with him but I think they whipped him quite good.

Now another story, very good friends of ours. They are living now in the States too. And the girls, friends over there too, aged maybe between five and six years. The girlfriend of the daughter of mine she was bitten by a dog. And then she had the doctor examinations and she had to go to Shanghai to the health department for shots against rabies. I brought the girls in. My wife was along and my wife was going with that friend of my daughter to get a shot and I was doing some shopping for my little tobacco store what I had and then we met again in Nanking Road, one of the very modern and business like streets in Shanghai. The whole street five or six big department stores, Wing-On, Sun-Sun, Sin and all the Chinese stores with ice skating rinks in it and department stores, ice skating rinks, and movie theater, and big dining room and dance hall, dancing halls. And one of this in Wing-On they had a little bit a coffee shop, like a coffee shop downstairs and I was willing to treat the girls and my wife to a cup of coffee. The girls had a cup of cacao and a little piece of cake and we were sitting there and the girlfriend of my daughter, she was enjoying it very much. The girls thought this was something really out of this world. Then when we were back at home and she was talking about this with her parents she said, "You wouldn't believe it! Notice each one had a cup with a handle on it. Everyone got his own coffee spoon." There is nothing else to say. That is the best picture in what fair condition we were living in Shanghai.

Neil: Trip over in the boat, just a little bit.

Manfred: I mean I was, we were before so far this we were getting our visa from the American Consulate and we were able to go to emigrate from China to America. There was plenty of work to it and plenty of commotion to it. This was an quite exciting, very exciting time. When we were taking that boat we had to pass Chinese customs because the Japanese were out already of Shanghai. They were transported to Japan after the war, after the whole war was over. So we had to pass Chinese customs, was very light and easy custom because eh, people were taking souvenirs from Shanghai this was true. So I was so happy.

Disc 4

Manfred: 7th session continued. So there were a lots of commotion. It was really a very exciting time. We were finally so far that we were able to board the transport boat which was bringing us from Shanghai to San Francisco. Uh, everybody was happy and everybody was lucky only the conditions were very rough because the name of the boat was General Meigs. They were transporting all the troops overseas in such boats. So we were leaving Shanghai we were going to Yokohama, Tokyo. We were able to go a little bit on land. We saw a little bit from Yokohama how that was bombed and there was nothing more standing and the whole thing was really down. We staying for a couple hours in Yokohama and then we were leaving for Hawaii.

We had a nice and quiet trip. We were excited. We had already American party customs on board and we had to fill out questionnaires and we had to ja, fill out questionnaires for usual because they were taking over of us in San Francisco. In Honolulu we had one day, one day stop from the morning to late nights before we were going on and we had a very nice day in Honolulu. The Jewish Welfare Fund had a club house in Hawaii. We were guest there. They were serving us a nice lunch and a nice dinner in the evenings. They were planning for us to pick buses ... And they were making three or four hour trips with us to show us all of Hawaii, Waikiki beach, and all the hotels and far out at the mountains. So we had a very nice day in Honolulu. We were going on to San Francisco. In San Francisco, we are leaving the boat before we passed customs which was quite awhile and then we had to, we met with very old friends.

Gerda in background.

Manfred: Okay we met old friends. And late in the afternoon, we are arriving early in the morning. Late afternoon we were free to go and we got hotel room.

Gerda: We were at Western.

Manfred (*lightly chuckles-audible smile*) We were at Western hotel. We stayed sixteen days in San Francisco. We were in Oakland. We saw Golden Gate. We saw Beebridge.

Gerda: I think it's called Bay Bridge.

Manfred: Bay Bridge downtown. Sixteen days sightseeing in San Francisco. From there we left for our destination. In the last six years I, were twice in San Francisco, all to remind us of what I had our beginning in America. I think now San Francisco is much better than it was twenty years ago when we arrived.

This is to end up the sessions. We are willing to rehear now the whole story and now maybe later on we have to put something on it.

II

Maps

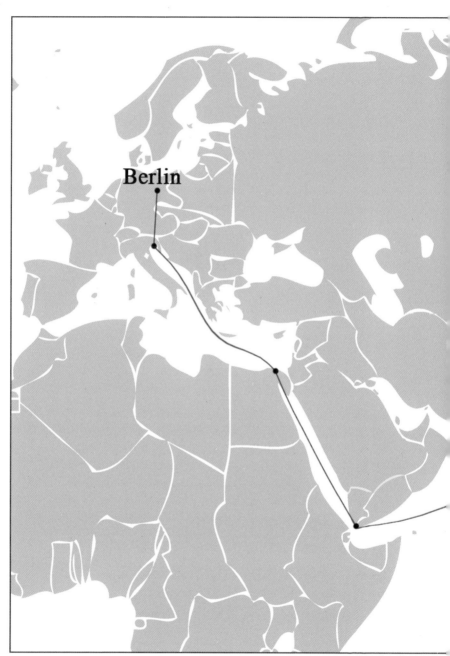

Map showing the route of the Conte Verde *from Berlin to Shanghai*

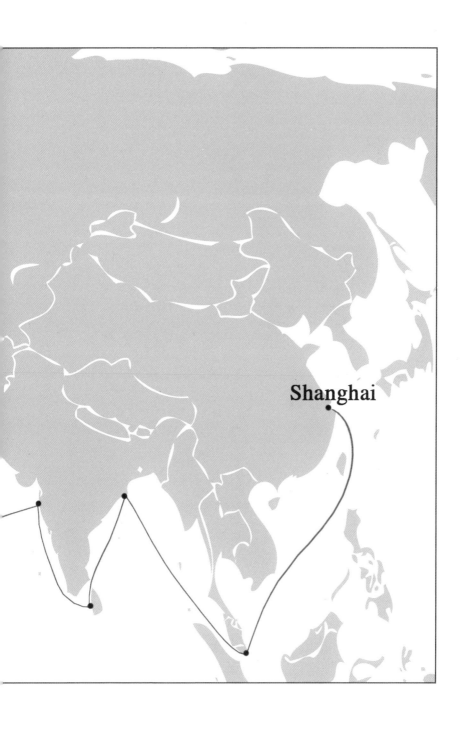
Shanghai

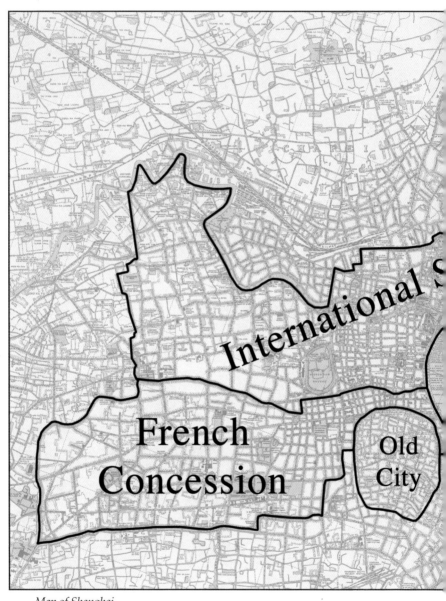

Map of Shanghai

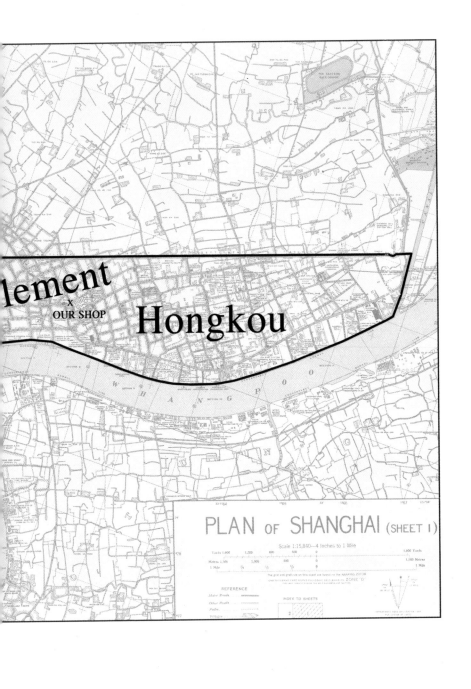

lement

x
OUR SHOP

Hongkou

W H A N G P O O

PLAN of SHANGHAI (SHEET 1)

Scale 1:15,840—4 Inches to 1 Mile

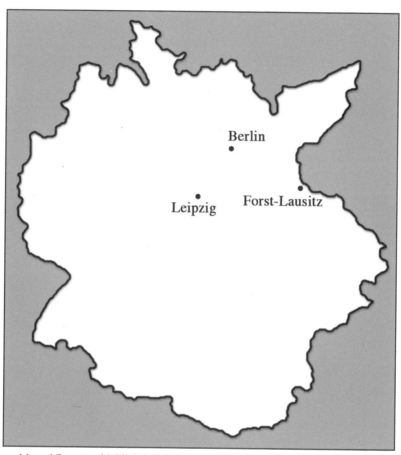

Map of Germany highlighting the cities pertinent to the Oelsners' story.

III

Index

Index